The ART of SPET

The ART of SPET

SPORTS PERFORMANCE ENHANCEMENT TRAINING

Stefan Shakiba, LMFT

Copyright © 2016 by Stefan Shakiba, LMFT

All rights reserved

Printed in the United States of America

First Edition

ISBN: 069276707X
ISBN 13: 9780692767078

Edited by Tyler Shores

Design Cover by Alexander Valchev

Special Consultant is Ben Liepman, MBA

Special Thanks to Cristina, Broderick, and Meredith

About the Author

Stefan Shakiba's blend of experience within the field of sports and as a Licensed Marriage and Family Therapist have helped pave the way for a revolutionary new approach to working with athletes. His integration of the latest tools and strategies to maximize mental soundness on the field makes *The Art of SPET* applicable and relevant for today's athletes. Many of his athletes have achieved considerable success, including getting recruited into college, being selected in the professional draft, and advancing within the professional ranks. His athletes include collegiate and professional athletes, including those at the Major League Baseball and Major League Soccer levels.

As a mental health clinician, Stefan is trained in multiple empirically-based clinical mental health treatment models. His areas of expertise include behavioral therapy, neuro-psychological assessments, trauma treatment, and intensive clinical interventions. Prior to becoming a therapist, Stefan spent the majority of his life as an athlete. He was a ranked tennis player in Northern California, competed for traveling teams in soccer and football, and played baseball for over two decades.

Stefan's sports experience extends beyond being an athlete. He was a high school tennis coach; conducted research for sports agents Steinberg Moorad and Dunn; served as the Director of Baseball Operations at the University of California, Berkeley; and consults with coaches in various sports to boost team morale and team cohesion. Given the breadth of his experience in both sports and psychology, he created *The Art of SPET* so coaches and sports professionals everywhere can help their athletes maximize performance.

Stefan earned his Bachelors degree from UC Berkeley, and holds Masters degrees from the University of San Francisco (Sports Management) and Pepperdine University (Clinical Psychology). He currently resides in Pasadena, California, where he continues to work both as a SPET coach and as a licensed therapist. Please enjoy the book. If you have any questions, or simply want to share your story, you may contact Stefan at theartofspet@gmail.com, or visit the website at artofspet.com.

Dedicated to Xavier and Oliver, may you always follow your heart and pursue your dreams.

Dedicated to Xavier and Oliver, may you always follow your heart and pursue your dreams.

Table of Contents

About the Author·· vii

Introduction··· xvii

Chapter 1　　Session 1: The Assessment Interview ························· 1
　　　　　　Why the assessment interview is so important ·········· 2
　　　　　　Issues regarding accuracy during the
　　　　　　assessment interview··································· 3
　　　　　　10 Critical Mental Skills································ 8
　　　　　　　　Critical Skill #1: Confidence························ 8
　　　　　　　　Critical Skill #2: Positive Self-Talk·················· 10
　　　　　　　　Critical Skill #3: Desire for Personal On-Field Success ··· 11
　　　　　　　　Critical Skill #4: Dedication and Commitment
　　　　　　　　　　to the Game······························· 12
　　　　　　　　Critical Skill #5: Competitive Edge (Spirit) ·········· 14
　　　　　　　　Critical Skill #6: Stress Management and
　　　　　　　　　　Coping Skills······························ 15
　　　　　　　　Critical Skill #7: Ability to Self-Motivate············ 17
　　　　　　　　Critical Skill #8: Passion for the Game ············· 20
　　　　　　　　Critical Skill #9: Ability to Focus··················· 21
　　　　　　　　Critical Skill #10: Personal Goal Setting ············ 22

Chapter 2	Session 2: Building a Road Map	23
	Overview of Session Two	23
	1: Review our Findings	24
	2: Introduction to SPET	24
	3: Education	25
	4: Goal Setting	27
	Overview of Goal Setting	27
	Recommended Guidelines for Goal Setting	27
	5: Predicting Game-Day Performance: Green Flags – Red Flags	31
	End of Session Two	33

Critical Mental Skills Targeted: Goal Setting, Dedication and Commitment to the Game

Chapter 3	Session 3: Stress Management and Coping Skills	34
	Overview of Session Three	34
	As the Start of Session Three	35
	Content of Session Three	36
	1: Mindfulness:	36
	Overview of Mindfulness	36
	The Bubblegum Mindfulness Exercise	37
	2: Deep Breathing	39
	Background	39
	How to Apply Deep Breathing	40
	After Practicing Deep Breathing	40
	3: Muscle Relaxation	41
	4: Grounding	42
	Background	42
	How to Apply Grounding	43
	After Grounding Exercises	44
	5: Guided Meditation	45
	Background	45

　　　　　　　How to Apply Guided Meditation · · · · · · · · · · · · · · · · · 45
　　　　　　　After Guided Imagery · 48
　　　　　　　End of Session Three · 48

Critical Mental Skills Targeted: Stress Management, Focusing Skills

Chapter 4　Session 4: Posititive Self-Talk and Positive Thinking · · · · · · · · · · 50
　　　　　　　Overview of Session Four · 50
　　　　　　　Start of Session Four · 50
　　　　　　　Content of Session Four · 52
　　　　　　　1: Thought Stopping · 52
　　　　　　　　　Background · 52
　　　　　　　　　How to Apply Thought Stopping · · · · · · · · · · · · · · · · · · 53
　　　　　　　2: Positive Self-Talk and Positive Thinking · · · · · · · · · · · · · · · 55
　　　　　　　　　Background · 55
　　　　　　　　　The Freud Game · 56
　　　　　　　　　Case Example of the Freud Game · · · · · · · · · · · · · · · · · 58
　　　　　　　　　After Practicing the Freud Game · · · · · · · · · · · · · · · · · · 59
　　　　　　　3: Flooding · 59
　　　　　　　　　Background · 59
　　　　　　　　　How to Apply Flooding · 61
　　　　　　　　　After Flooding · 63
　　　　　　　End of Session Four · 64

Critical Mental Skills Targeted: Positive Self-Talk, Focusing, Confidence, Ability to Self-Motivate, Desire for On-Field Success

Chapter 5　Session 5: Poise and Behavior Control · 65
　　　　　　　Overview of Session Five · 65
　　　　　　　Start of Session Five · 66
　　　　　　　Content of Session Five · 67
　　　　　　　1: Poise Education · 67
　　　　　　　　　Positive Signs of Poise · 67

Negative Signs of Poise 68
All-Around Poise 69
An Example Highlighting the Importance of
the Mind-Body Connection 70
2: Knowing Our Triggers 71
Triggers 71
3: All-around Poise Control Practice 72
Case Example 73
End of Session Five 75

Critical Mental Skills Targeted: Stress Management, Positive Self-Talk, Confidence, Focusing, Ability to Self-Motivate, Competitive Edge

Chapter 6 Session 6: The Imagery Experience 76
Overview of Session Six 76
At the Start of Session Six 77
Content of Session Six 78
1: Positive Imagery 78
Case Example 80
2: Sensory-Integrated-Imagery-Training 82
What is Sensory-Integrated-Imagery-Training 82
Why Sensory-Integrated-Imagery-Training 83
Where Athletes Can Practice Sensory-
Integrated-Imagery-Training 84
Scenarios for Sensory-Integrated-Imagery-Training 85
Preparing for Sensory-Integrated-Imagery-Training 86
How to Apply Sensory-Integrated-Imagery-Training ... 88
Case Example 89
End of Session Six 94

Critical Mental Skills Targeted: Stress Management, Positive Self-Talk, Confidence, Focusing, Ability to Self-motivate, Competitive Edge, Dedication and Commitment to the Game

Chapter 7	Session 7: Skills Review and Prevention Planning············95
	Overview of Session Seven ······························95
	At the Start of Session Seven····························96
	Content of Session Seven ·································97
	1: Re-Assess Newly Strengthened Critical Mental Skills ·····97
	2: Goal Outcomes··98
	3: Reviewing Green Flags and Red Flags ················99
	4: Skills Review ··99
	5: Prevention Planning·································· 100
	End of Session Seven ····································101

Chapter 8	Band-Aid Strategies·· 102
	What are Band-Aids ···································· 102
	Confidence ·· 103
	A Reality-Check ···································· 103
	Highlight Continual Progress ·····················104
	Showing Attitude··································· 105
	The Golden Gift Theory ·························· 105
	Desire for Personal On-Field Success ··················106
	Remembering How Success Felt···················106
	"Reverse Psychology" ····························· 107
	Dedication and Commitment to the Game ············109
	Learning From The Best···························109
	Competitive Edge ······································· 110
	Listing Strengths··································· 110
	Ability to Self-Motivate: ·······························111
	Self Reflection ····································111
	Mirroring other Athletes ··························111
	Comparing Debbie Downer to Positive Pat········ 112
	Passion for the Game···································· 113
	Internal Triggers, Internal Solutions;
	External Triggers, External Solutions·············· 113
	Putting Things into Perspective ·················· 115

Ability to Focus · 115
   Rapid Eye-Movement · 115
   Stimulating the Five Senses · 116
   Focusing on a specific object: · 118
   Sing a Song, Think of Something Funny · · · · · · · · · · · 119
   Explore Extracurricular Focusing Activities · · · · · · · · · 120
Final Words: · 120

Introduction

When an athlete rows one side of a boat by themselves, they go in circles. But when we sit beside them and paddle at the same time, we move forward.

Many coaches have heard of the different techniques athletes can use to improve mental performance on the field. We often hear how important it is to use positive self-talk, relaxation skills, positive imagery, and so on. Yet we are often left with many unanswered questions; questions such as where do we start, how do we apply certain strategies, and when should we apply certain strategies. If we're unsure how to proceed, the process can be confusing. I created *the ART of SPET* to answer these questions and to prepare coaches to maximize an athlete's mental toughness on the field. This model really works. It will help good athletes get better. And it will help great athletes become greater.

In reality, solidifying the mental game takes time. While some athletes will benefit from quick-fix solutions, most will require weeks if not months before they solidify mental soundness. *The Art of SPET* is designed to address both temporary and chronic issues. It teaches anyone working with athletes everything they need to know to build mental resiliency on the field. It is a one-stop-shop organized so it is easy-to-follow and maximizes results. This way, when adversity strikes on the field, athletes will be fully capable of tackling any mental performance obstacle independently in the future.

The *Art of SPET* will change how you think about sports psychology. Whether you're a team coach, SPET Coach, Sports Psychologist, Strength and Conditioning coach, personal trainer, physical therapist, an agent, scout, or even a parent, anyone who interacts with athletes will benefit from what this book has to offer. *The Art of SPET* is written as a step-by-step, beginning-to-end process, but is very flexible in its application. Your relationship with athletes will determine how you apply the information.

For those using this model in its entirety, I refer to you throughout the book as a *SPET Coach (Sports Performance Enhancement Trainer)*. For SPET coaches, chapters one through seven represent individual sessions, usually about one hour per session. Each subsequent chapter builds upon the skills from the previous chapter, so athletes progressively master each skill before moving on to the next. Using this format will produce exceptional results. Results you will be proud of.

As for team coaches, you will have many more options on how to apply SPET tools and techniques. Whether it's pinpointing a player's mental weakness, plucking out specific strategies to improve individual player needs, getting the most out of your star player, or applying weekly strategies using a group format, you have the luxury of helping individual athletes and the entire team alike. Moreover, you have the option of creating "mini-packages" that mix-and-match different strategies to concoct individualized formulas for each athlete. Here, the possibilities are limitless.

As for everyone else using *The Art of SPET*, your newfound knowledge will certainly make you more marketable and expand what you have to offer athletes. Your athletes will appreciate that. For example, a physical fitness trainer may teach a client how to find their "runner's high" quicker. A strength and conditioning coach may teach an athlete how to self-motivate in an attempt to break their previous deadlift record. Or a scout may recruit athletes who are more mentally sound and better equipped to compete at the next level.

Before we dive in and discuss powerful mental enhancement strategies, chapter one will review ten "critical mental skills" we should consider. I call these mental skills "critical" because based on my research and experience they represent common mental traits shared by the majority of successful athletes. Identifying the ten critical mental skills will be important because they will reveal exactly what athletes need to improve.

In the final chapter of this book (chapter eight) I offer supplemental mental enhancement strategies which I call "Band-Aids." Band-Aid strategies are designed to target specific critical mental skills, and can be incorporated into the SPET process at any time. When we combine Band-Aids into the SPET process, athletes will improve critical mental skills quicker. I call these strategies "Band-Aids" because they were initially designed to stop the bleeding when athletes experience urgent performance issues. Incorporating Band-Aids allows us to customize our approach for each athlete. And they provide us with dozens of additional tools to consider. I am certain you will find these Band-Aid strategies useful.

Athletes may ask whether *The Art of SPET* is effective as a self-help guide. Theoretically, the answer is yes. When athletes incorporate SPET strategies into their routines they should experience results. However, athletes must approach certain strategies with caution considering some of the strategies require the assistance from a coach. Some strategies involve dually integrated role-plays to achieve optimal results. Others require important feedback from coaches to help athletes progressively fine-tune their skills. While this book has a lot to offer athletes, it is primarily intended for coaches and sports professionals.

You may notice that many of the case examples I provide involve baseball players. Baseball happens to be my specialty. The good news is SPET techniques are relevant to all sports. So when I describe a baseball player harnessing his focus, athletes in golf, football, soccer, basketball, and tennis can use the same tools to achieve similar results. It will be up to you and the athlete to decide how best to apply these strategies given the unique nature of each sport. Enjoy the book!

CHAPTER 1

Session 1: The Assessment Interview

"Ricky" was an accomplished pitcher at the Division I collegiate baseball level who sported a low 90's fastball, supported by a nasty change-up and curveball. Success came easy to Ricky at the college level with his six-foot-two, two-hundred pound frame, as he was selected in the Major League Draft. Despite a dominant first year of professional baseball, early into his second season Ricky's performance began to dive while playing in high-A ball. Ricky's struggles began to frustrate him, leading to a continued downward spiral in performance. After over a month of struggling, during which time Ricky amassed an earned run average of over five, Ricky became desperate, picked up his phone, and made an important phone call.

Before making that important phone call, stories like Ricky's are far more common than many people realize. Talent alone doesn't guarantee success on the field. Even gifted athletes are subject to mental performance issues at some point in their careers. You'll rarely see athletes go directly up to their head coach and open up about an issue, let alone see a rookie do it. When a crisis arises, it's important for athletes to have someone safe to confide in; someone they can trust who will not punish them for their disclosure. When an athlete reaches out to us for help, we should always greet them with open arms. Sometimes performance barriers arise when athletes are forced to adjust to new transitions, such as while moving up the ranks, or adjusting to unfamiliar environments. Athletes who have sound mental skills have an easier time adapting to new challenges and situations. Unfortunately, there are many athletes like Ricky who never truly faced adversity before, and therefore never made it a priority to develop their mental game.

In this chapter we will discuss where to start when someone like Ricky approaches us for help. The assessment interview will become our guide as we help him get back on track and give him the best chance to succeed on the field. In this chapter we will accomplish three goals: to review the purpose of the assessment interview; to highlight issues regarding accuracy during the assessment interview; and to introduce the ten *critical mental skills* that will help us determine how to maximize mental performance on the field.

Why the assessment interview is so important

The assessment interview is the ideal opportunity to collect all the information we need before working on actual mental skills building with athletes like Ricky. During this time we want to gather all the relevant information up front, and avoid missing out on key factors negatively impacting on-field performance. As a clinical therapist, fully understanding the scope of a problem from the very beginning makes it easier to identify which interventions to consider. Working with athletes is similar because knowing exactly what is positively and negatively impacting them will determine which strategies we will rely on the most to bring out their full potential.

Exploring and assessing for the ten *critical mental skills* will be a major focus as we help athletes improve mental performance on the field. By identifying which *critical mental skills* represent mental strengths, and which *critical mental skills* represent areas for improvement, we will get an accurate snapshot into their current situation. This will reveal their individual performance needs. We will use mental strengths to their advantage, by encouraging athletes to rely on and build around these strengths.

We will target weaker mental skills to not only stop them from impeding performance, but to potentially turn them into assets. The ART of SPET is a combination one-size-fits-all approach *and* an individualized approach. It offers guidelines on how to target individual strengths and areas for improvement depending on where an athlete currently stands. Band-Aid strategies are additionally useful to further customize our approach for each athlete.

As a side note to working with athletes, I always prefer to refer to mental "weaknesses" as "areas for improvement." Positive wording avoids negative connotations and sends a powerful and clear message that an athlete is capable of improving weaker mental skills.

Issues regarding accuracy during the assessment interview

There are several important issues regarding accuracy of information coaches and sports professionals need to consider during the assessment interview. First is the issue of *trust*. When we meet with athletes to address mental skills, we could reasonably expect some athletes to be initially reserved or uncomfortable answering our questions in depth. We typically notice this when athletes respond to our questions with short answers or brief responses. This is understandable because exposing a mental area for improvement can be a sensitive subject leading to demoralization. Some athletes may be unaware they lack certain mental skills or have never explored the possibility. Others may worry their information will be disclosed to others, leading them to either hide or exaggerate the current status of mental skills. Before we assess for critical mental skills we want to take proactive steps to build trust.

To promote honesty and accuracy during the assessment, I always begin by broaching the issue of trust. When we feel trust, we are far more likely to be open and honest with others. When we feel distrust, we tend to put our guard up by withholding important information due to feelings of emotional vulnerability. The last thing anyone wants is to be judged or perceived as "damaged goods" for being honest. Athletes typically express relief when I guarantee a 100% non-judgmental environment because this is what they want to hear. They need to feel safe knowing we are on their side, and that through self-awareness and insight we will use the information in their best interest.

As we continue to address the topic of trust, this would be the ideal time to disclose our policy regarding *confidentiality*. Confidentiality is a component of trust. Confidentiality restricts how much of the athlete's information we may or may not share with others. My policy regarding confidentiality is to withhold all of the athlete's information without their expressed signed consent. This means everything they open up to me about will remain a complete secret unless they give me written permission to share information. I also make it a policy to never disclose the names of athletes I have worked with in the past (including name-dropping). This too is intended to protect their privacy. A strong policy on confidentiality, in the athlete's favor, fosters a safe emotional environment where athletes can express themselves freely without any fears of repercussion or embarrassment.

A second issue related to accuracy during the assessment interview includes the phenomenon of *over-reporting* and *under-reporting*. Over-reporting typically occurs when an athlete over-exaggerates a specific critical mental skill in order to maintain confidence or ego levels. In my experience younger athletes are more likely to over-exaggerate critical mental strengths compared to older, more experienced athletes. While I am generally not concerned when athletes tell me they have an exceptional critical mental strength, over-reporting can become problematic if we automatically assume a critical mental skill is strong, when in fact that "strength" requires significant improvement. In this case, by mistakenly assuming an athlete has a significant critical mental skill, we are actually setting them up for potential failure by failing to address a key issue. Here it gets a little tricky because while athletes generally have nothing to hide from SPET coaches, they potentially have a lot more to lose if they open up to a team coach who has influence over playing time. For team coaches, the stronger the trust between you and your players, the more likely they will reach out to you for help. If you tell athletes to "suck it up," or minimize what they have to say by brushing their problem off, you will probably find your roster filled with insecure over-reporters.

Under-reporting typically occurs when an athlete minimizes a critical mental skill or reports that a specific critical mental skill is a non-issue. Unlike over-reporting, an athlete may under-report a critical mental skill because they are simply unaware or are in denial about it. If we fail to accurately identify areas for improvement, weaker mental skills can linger during their athletic career and never get resolved. As coaches and sports professionals, we want to give athletes the best shot at succeeding by preventing negative cycles from recurring.

To monitor for over-reporting and under-reporting we can use a *checks-and-balances* approach as we measure each critical mental skill. I use four specific checks-and-balances techniques to search for clues and inconsistencies indicating potential inaccuracies of critical mental skill levels. These checks-and-balances techniques are easy to apply. The first method is by rephrasing the same questions to see if I get different answers the next time. If I reword the same question several times only to get conflicting responses, a "red flag" goes up in my head indicating that what they are telling us does not match up. For example, to gauge competitive spirit I may ask "how often do you enjoy competing?" and, "are there times when you don't enjoy competing?" If an athlete answers the first questions with "I love to compete all the time!" but then answers the second question with "Yeah, there are times when it's not fun," things don't match up. Usually what happens in these cases is athletes impulsively answer a question without taking the time to think it through. When this occurs, we need to ask additional follow-up questions to gauge critical mental skills more accurately.

A second checks-and-balances method is by asking for specific examples in the past when athletes used a critical mental skill to their advantage, and times when critical mental skills ultimately hurt their performance. By reviewing their performance history we can compare whether their insight into critical mental skills match up with reality. When we notice inconsistencies between past performance and current opinions, there may be over- or under-reporting going on. For example, if an athlete says they're always confident, but have thoughts of self-doubt during certain situations, things don't match up. In cases when athletes give us vague responses, or cannot offer specific examples highlighting certain critical mental skills, there is a good chance mental skills need improvement. If athletes can back up critical mental skills with relevant examples from the past, they are more likely to be on point.

A third checks-and-balances method involves offering hypothetical, on-field scenarios to explore how critical mental skills may impact performance in the future. These hypothetical scenarios may include questions such as "how would you keep your body relaxed in 'X' situation," "what thoughts would cross your mind in 'Y' situation," or "how would you remain motivated during times of struggle." In these examples we are assessing an athlete's stress management skills, thinking patterns, and ability to self-motivate. When an athlete gives a satisfactory account into how they would handle a hypothetical situation, mental skills may be stronger. If an athlete has a hard time telling us which steps they would take to handle the situation, we should explore critical mental skills further to determine if it needs improvement.

Offering hypothetical scenarios serves an additional purpose as well. They give us valuable insight into whether athletes currently use specific mental performance techniques. When athletes mention using specific techniques on the field, critical skills are more likely to be stronger because they already have some tools to rely on. On the other hand, when athletes are unable to mention specific techniques, they may have greater difficulty maintaining critical mental skills on the field. The more techniques they already use, the better prepared they are at managing difficult situations. The fewer techniques they use, the quicker we need to get them up to speed by teaching them about the strategies which already exist.

The fourth checks-and-balances technique is the most common approach. It involves addressing inconsistencies face-to-face. This offers athletes the chance to clarify our confusion and to think more critically about their actual situation. Gently confronting them about inconsistencies promotes insight and awareness. After all, we are providing athletes with a safe emotional environment where they are encouraged to look more deeply inside themselves. Getting them to buy-in about the importance of improving their insight (and making us aware of what's going on) will only help them in the long run.

In some cases athletes will confirm what they originally told us. In other cases athletes may admit feelings of embarrassment, disappointment, or even shame. In the case of the latter, this would be a good time to normalize their emotions given that for many of us, feeling vulnerable is uncomfortable. I always praise athletes for divulging new insights in order to continue encouraging openness and to promote trust. By eventually acknowledging needed areas for improvement athletes show us courage. Before I actually begin assessing for critical mental skills, I always reassure athletes that strengthening mental skills is a process and a very realistic goal. I say this to instill hope, and to inspire them to commit to using the strategies we teach.

To simplify the checks-and-balances process, I have created a basic checklist you may consider using while assessing for accuracy of each critical mental skill. This checklist includes the first three checks-and-balances techniques previously discussed, each numbered one through three. As you assess for individual critical mental skills, if you mark "yes" to any of the checks-and-balances techniques below, you can use the fourth checks-and-balances approach by addressing the issue directly with athletes for further clarification.

Critical Mental Skills:

1: Are there inconsistent responses regarding a mental skill?
 (yes)   (no)
2: Does performance history match-up to athlete's reports?
 (yes)   (no)
3: Can the athlete walk you through hypothetical situations?
 (yes)   (no)

10 Critical Mental Skills

Based on my research and extensive time working with athletes, I have identified 10 specific mental skills we should always assess for. In baseball I refer to these skills as "the sixth tool" (hitting for average, power, arm strength, base running, and fielding ability are the other five-tools). It's equally important for scouts, recruiters, and front office staff to gauge critical mental skills in prospective athletes so they know whether athletes are mentally prepared to play at the next level. Scouts and recruiters may subtly ask athletes questions measuring critical mental skills, such as: "How much time do you spend training *off* the field (this measures commitment and dedication)?" "What is your secret to focusing on the field (whether true or not)?" Or "what do your teammates say about your motivational style?" Afterwards, by comparing their word from their action you will have a better idea into what type of player you are dealing with.

As we review each critical mental skill, you may notice a lot of overlap between them. Each mental skill can have a direct impact on others. For example, the ability to remain positive can impact self-motivation abilities. Passion for the game may inspire dedication and commitment. And a competitive edge may support confidence.

To assess which critical mental skills are strengths, and which represent areas for improvement, I use a rating scale to measure each skill. Using a rating scale from one through five makes gauging each skill easier. A score of "1" on the scale means a mental skill needs serious improvement. A score of "5" on the scale means a mental skill is a serious strength. Scores four and above represent strengths. Any score under four means a mental skill needs improvement.

Critical Skill #1: Confidence

Confidence is when athletes believe their talents and strengths are good enough to achieve success on the field. The more we are successful, the more we believe in ourselves. Examples when we are most confident include when we have a long track record of success and during hot streaks. In these situations we are riding a wave of momentum to continually pull us forward. Whether we are facing a really tough opponent or are having a bad game, confidence transcends these barriers that may otherwise inhibit success. Confidence is about trusting yourself, supported by positive self-talk and self-motivational skills. If an athlete tells his or herself "I believe" over and over again, they probably will end up believing. However, when athletes express self-doubt they are more likely to buy into negative feeling and thinking patterns, thereby tarnishing their confidence.

Athletes who struggle with confidence compete with a damaged mindset. The collateral effects can be crippling, potentially leading to: reduced motivation; increased negative thinking; lapses in focus; reduced intensity and competitive spirit; and a loss of physical composure. When athletes start doubting themselves they tend to approach new situations by prematurely forecasting a negative outcome. This can inevitably doom them to failure. If an athlete says "I don't think I can beat this guy," their lack of confidence turns into a disadvantage for them and an enormous advantage for their opponent. If we know our opponent is intimidated by us, instinctively we will experience a boost in confidence knowing our talents are intimidation-worthy.

There is an obvious correlation between natural talent and confidence. The stronger and faster the athlete, the more they can rely on their physical advantages to overcome challenging circumstances. Unfortunately, when athletes rely too heavily on their physical strengths alone, the more susceptible they are to eventual mental breakdown. This is especially true for athletes who stood out as an amateur, a time when physical superiority typically trump the mental strengths of their opponents. As athletes move up the ranks within their sport, where the talent level begins to even out, self-confidence can get tested. Athletes with a sound mental game are more likely to persevere when the going gets tough compared to athletes who previously didn't have to rely on their mental game to achieve success. This is a big reason why many professional athletes approach me for help: persistent struggles against a new pool of talent can challenge preexisting confidence. This is largely what happened to Ricky whom we will continue to discuss in a moment.

When we assess for confidence it is important to consider confidence is one of the more sensitive critical mental skills, thus more difficult to measure. In fact, confidence is more likely to be either under-reported or over-reported because it is a fragile topic. Some athletes may be unaware they lack confidence. Some may be in denial about their confidence. Others may be too ashamed to admit their confidence is an issue. As we assess for confidence, this would be a great time to apply our checks-and-balances tools to monitor for accurate confidence levels.

You may notice that as we help athletes reinforce their mental game, their confidence will naturally develop accordingly as stronger mental skills are relied upon to achieve on-field results. To further promote confidence building, I highly suggest incorporating Band-Aid strategies from the get-go to build confidence quicker.

Critical Skill #2: Positive Self-Talk

Positive self-talk is a second critical mental skill successful careered athletes share. Positive self-talk is generally sparked by positive feelings and has hopeful connotations associated with them. Examples of positive self-talk include "I can" or "I will" statements. Athletes who use positive self-talk have an easier time self-motivating during hard times. When athletes tell themselves "I can do this," they will feel more optimistic and hopeful about their situation.

Negative self-talk statements tend to be fueled by negative feelings (i.e. frustration or disappointment), and often imply "don't do this," "I won't," or "I can't" attitudes. When athletes use negative self-talk they are expressing self-doubt, thereby essentially forecasting a negative outcome. One of the dangers of negative self-talk is it can become habit forming if not addressed early. I often compare negative self-talk to cancer: if either is not treated early, they can spread and eventually become overwhelming and unmanageable. This is why it is so important to accurately assess an athlete's positive and negative thinking patterns from the beginning in order to prevent a malignant (cancerous) spiral.

For the most part, negative self-talk is what I call "UHU": *unhelpful, hurtful*, and *unnecessary*. For the majority of athletes, UHU statements serve no useful purpose. Fortunately, athletes can improve positive thinking patterns through practice, practice, and more practice.

Self-talk can include both *external* and *internal* statements. Each is important. External self-talk statements are said aloud, intentionally directed towards others to hear. Internal self-talk statements are said to one's self and are not meant to be shared with others. Differentiating between external and internal statements is important because what an athlete communicates verbally to teammates and coaches may not truly reflect what they are actually thinking and feeling inside. Faked positive external statements may be said due to social pressure to remain positive by teammates. Perhaps far more common are faked positive external statements said around coaches to avoid being scolded, criticized, or benched. By understanding internal self-talk patterns, we will gain better insight into an athlete's true thinking patterns. Since positive self-talk is such an important skill, improving positive thinking patterns will be the entire focus of chapter four.

Critical Skill #3: Desire for Personal On-Field Success

Many athletes have a natural ambition to be successful on the field. The definition of personal success will vary from one athlete to the next. Some may define personal on-field success based on statistics, tenure, level of play, awards received, quality of performance, salary, and so on. When we assess a desire for personal success, we want to hone in specifically onto on-field performance rather than all the perks associated with being an athlete. Athletes who want to be the best typically go the extra mile to gain an advantage over their opponents. NBA All-Star Stephen Curry is a great example. He's stated on multiple occasions he wants to be the best he can be at basketball. Curry can flawlessly dribble two basketballs at the same time and drain 3-pointers from well behind the arc, making it look easy. This doesn't just happen overnight. Curry harvested his talents over time to reach this potential because he knew he was capable of it. When athletes have an authentic desire to be the best, they are more likely to have superior work ethics, continually strive towards improving their routines, and respect the game knowing it takes time to master. Athletes who are hungry for personal success often show more intensity and focus when they compete, as does Curry.

Nearly every athlete will report they want to be successful on the field. Very few will say they are satisfied with mediocrity. Yet when athletes say one thing, unsupported by their actual work ethic, their desire for personal success may come into question. When ambitions do not match efforts we want to point out these conflicting messages to promote awareness and insight into their situation. This empowers athletes to make a conscious decision. They can either change their habits to match their desire for personal on-field success. Or they can continue engaging in the same patterns that limited their performance in the first place. Proposing these two options helps athletes prioritize what is most important to them.

Critical Skill #4: Dedication and Commitment to the Game

Dedication and commitment to the game is an important critical mental skill directly linked to a desire for personal success. When we mentally want something really bad we are more likely to physically act on it. Dedication and commitment is the actual follow-through based on one's ambition. It has to do with the depth, breadth, and scope of an athlete's work ethic both on and off the field. Dedication and commitment is inspired by positive self-talk, self-motivational skills, one's desire to compete, and their passion for the game. I consider dedication and commitment to the game a mental skill because we as coaches can make a real impact here. While some of us may not have the technical expertise to work on an athlete's physical mechanics, we definitely hold the influence to inspire them to work harder. Athletes who are committed and dedicated to their sport typically go above and beyond the rest to hone their talents to the max.

There are two ways to measure an athlete's dedication and commitment. The first is by asking them to rate their work ethic on and off the field.

The second is by asking them to describe their actual work ethic in detail. Once we have gathered these bits of information we can begin comparing their talk and action. When athletes go on and on about their intensive practice routines, they are likely describing great dedication and commitment to their sport. But when athletes describe your "average Joe" routine, we want them to understand the implications of such a routine. We want athletes to understand that if they truly want to take their game to the next level, their dedication and commitment levels need to improve. Bringing this to their attention can inspire athletes to restructure their approach and take extra steps to match their desires with action.

Athletes who continually work towards maximizing their talents are far more likely to sustain a higher level of play. Their work ethic during non-game situations often translates into performance on game days. In many cases, athletes with intense work ethics can overachieve, especially those who are smaller, slower, or perhaps less talented. In other cases, exceptional work ethics can propel athletes to legendary status. When we look at the majority of the greatest athletes of all time, we will notice a blend of tremendous talent along with a remarkable work ethic. Michael Jordan. Michael Phelps. Serena Williams. Usain Bolt. Tiger Woods. Wayne Gretzky. NBA superstar Kobe Bryant was a poster child for dedication and commitment to the game of basketball. Along with training a minimum of four hours a day, Kobe was committed to maintaining a strict diet and continuously studied film. Kobe was notorious for waking up his trainers in the early morning because he was determined to get to the gym before anyone else.

Athletes who lack dedication and commitment are more susceptible to shorter careers. It's important for athletes to understand that no matter how hard they work toward improving their game, in most cases there will always be someone else who works harder than them. Athletes with inferior work ethics are far more likely to struggle with inconsistency on the field because they haven't taken the appropriate steps to remain competitive. When dedication is neglected, athletes can set themselves up for being benched, traded, or outright dropped from the roster. We've seen this over the years with many first-round-draft athletes in the major US sports. They were just as physically gifted as the other players, yet they were still unable to compete at the professional level.

An example of someone who lacked a commitment and dedication to the game of football includes Johnny Manziel, the former Cleveland Browns Quarterback in the NFL. Based on his actions off the field, it could be reasonably assumed that Manziel prioritized partying over improving as a passer. Although he did experience moderate success over a short period time, one can only imagine what he could have achieved had he embodied the dedication and commitment of someone who was successful, such as a Peyton Manning.

Athletes with tremendous talent who fail tend to have three things going against them: their talent alone was not enough; their work ethic was forgettable; and on the bench was an eager teammate who took their sport more seriously. When there are multiple big fish in a small pond, teams have options, including the option to eventually go with someone who is more driven.

Critical Skill #5: Competitive Edge (Spirit)

I think of competitive edge as an athlete's mental competitive spirit. This includes their attitudes about competing, their level of enjoyment when they compete, and the intensity they bring onto the field. When athletes show a strong competitive edge it is obvious even to an outside observer. Their purposeful eye gaze. Their stoic composure. Their intense focus. These athletes always want to be a part of the action no matter what the situation. They are not easily intimidated given the magnitude of a situation. Rather, they embrace pressure and seem to transcend their game to a whole other level. NBA player LeBron James is a great example. When things get tight and the game is on the line, he's the one who wants the ball. He's the one who teammates often rely on to get the job done in the closing seconds. He along with Michael Jordan are the epitome of clutch because they are intensely competitive and focused on winning.

Some athletes have the competitive spirit in their DNA. This is a tremendous asset. They typically have stubborn personality types and are always fiercely competitive both on and off the field. Whether it's playing a game of dominos with friends, or an innocent game of darts, they tend to get caught up in the moment and take competition very seriously. Even for those athletes who are only competitive on the field, they always have a reason to compete. Their motivations may be for different reason, such as for bragging rights, personal fulfillment, the thrill of victory, hating to lose, pride, or merely wanting to be the best they can be. This is why as we assess for competitive edge we want to find out what inspires athletes at any moment in the game.

Athletes who lack a competitive edge tend to show up to the field with a mindset of "we'll see what happens," as opposed to "I'm going to give them hell today!" This type of mentality sets athletes up for potential mental skills breakdown, including: negative self-talk, personal doubt, a loss in focus, and confidence issues. Fortunately, in many cases a reduction in competitive spirit can be rekindled by building around other mental skills. As athletes begin re-experiencing success, the more positive they will feel about competing.

Critical Skill #6: Stress Management and Coping Skills

Knowing when athletes experience stress and how they manage stress is a significant part of the assessment process. When we feel stress (including anxiety and nervousness), the hormones cortisol and epinephrine (aka adrenalin) are released into our bodies, causing an instant flight, fight, or freeze response reaction within us. Some athletes have the natural ability to keep these uncomfortable reactions in check. Others rely on relaxation and stress management skills to physically calm their bodies down. For many athletes, adrenalin hormones have an adverse effect because they cause muscles to tighten up, thereby impeding control of physical arm and leg movements. This can make it harder for athletes to execute basic mechanics. Public speaking is a great analogy of how stress can impact us. In front of large crowds, fears of embarrassing one's self increases physical stress symptoms through the release of cortisol and epinephrine. These hormones in turn increase the likelihood of uncontrollable bodily functions, including trembling, feeling weak in the knees, sweating, shortness of breath, rapid heartbeat, light headedness, muscle tension, fidgetiness, and stuttering. Fortunately, public speakers and athletes alike can use relaxation skills to reduce the physical effects of stress and reassert greater control over their bodies.

Athletes who use relaxation and coping skills to tolerate stress are significantly more likely to make free throws during the closing seconds, complete a pass on fourth down, make a penalty kick, and throw strikes on a full count. In football, "icing the kicker" is a common strategy used by coaches. By calling a time-out just before a field goal attempt, coaches are hoping the more time a kicker has to think about the magnitude of the situation, the more likely he will succumb to physical stress and miss the attempt. Stress management is absolutely essential in tennis and golf, where even the slightest tension in muscles can affect strokes; strokes which already require tremendous precision. In the case of Ricky, whom we discussed at the beginning of this chapter, his stress symptoms had become so unmanageable and overwhelming that he lost all confidence in his talents. By teaching Ricky to relax his body, along with rebuilding a positive mindset, Ricky was eventually able to regain full physical and mental control. He began experiencing renewed confidence. The following year he was promoted to Double-A ball.

Stress can be experienced in different ways, including physiologically (physically) and psychologically (mentally). Teaching athletes to identify their unique stress symptoms will let us know exactly which strategies they can rely on to target specific symptoms:

Physiological (physical) symptoms include:

- Increased heart rate
- Increased blood pressure
- Lightheadedness
- Sweating
- Muscle tension
- Fidgetiness

- Shaking or Trembling
- Reduced control of muscle movements
- Increased on-field mistakes or errors
- A loss of composure

Psychological symptoms (mental symptoms) include:

- Reduced confidence
- Inattention
- Distractibility
- Increased self-doubt
- Negative feelings (i.e. frustration, disappointment, fear, etc)
- Increased negative self-talk
- Reduced focus
- Overthinking

As we assess for stress management and coping skills we want to explore when athletes feel vulnerable to stress on the field. This includes identifying current stress triggers (situations that instigate stress today), past stress triggers, and anticipated stress triggers. Any triggers reported to us (either past, current, or anticipated) can be incorporated into the SPET process during upcoming meetings with athletes. This will give them the opportunity to build physical and mental resiliency to these situations in case they ever re-arise in the future.

Critical Skill #7: Ability to Self-Motivate

The ability to self-motivate is a powerful mental skill successful athletes use to remain competitive regardless of the situation. Self-motivation is directly linked to positive self-talk, which typically entails optimistic and hopeful attitudes. These athletes can overcome new struggles more quickly because they tend to perceive the next opportunity as a new opportunity to succeed. Whether an athlete is riding a hot streak, or in a slump, those who know how to self-motivate are far more likely to remain competitive at all times because they have the skills to remain inspired.

Athletes with less developed motivational abilities are more likely to obsess over recent struggles and mistakes. When athletes get consumed with negative thoughts, feelings, and emotions, it becomes harder to mentally rebound. This can create a snowball of additional struggles if they cannot mentally regroup and get their heads back in the game. Fortunately, there are many Band-Aid strategies to choose from which can provide immediate relief in case athletes are having a tough time self-motivating.

As we assess for self-motivational abilities, we want to know if and how athletes self-motivated in the past. This includes identifying times when they were able to inspire themselves immediately after an error or mistake. It also includes identifying times when athletes were unable to inspire themselves so we may work to prevent a similar reoccurrence later on down the road. Exploring how quickly athletes can motivate themselves is also important. The quicker they can self-motivate, the stronger the skill. The longer it takes to self-motivate, the more the skill needs improvement.

Exploring an athlete's on-field poise (physical composure) and individual mannerisms are ways we can visually measure self-motivational potential. These are behavioral tendencies team coaches must be aware of. The last thing coaches want is to put a player in the game who is not ready to be there, or leave a player in too long when they are exhibiting behavioral signs of emotional struggle (the latter happens far too often, especially when it comes to pitchers in baseball). Since the body is controlled by the mind, unusual or suspicious changes in physical behavior typically imply the mind is distracted and unhappy. Gauging physical composure is easier compared to identifying changes in individual mannerisms because a loss in poise is usually more obvious to the outside observer. When athletes visually lose their poise (i.e. swearing, yelling, slamming a piece of equipment, throwing tantrums, etc), we are witnessing their internal struggle given their loss of physical control. On the other hand, athletes who are able to maintain their poise are demonstrating a greater degree of control over their thoughts and feelings. These athletes will have a much easier time re-motivating themselves.

Changes in individual mannerisms are far more subtle to detect, yet represent compelling warning signs that something is up. Part of the reason why changes in mannerisms are easily overlooked is because even most athletes are unaware they are engaging in these behaviors. Athletes can proactively retain their physical composure to show coaches things are fine, even whey they are not. Hiding mannerisms is significantly more difficult because they often represent an unconscious behavior athletes are unaware of. Think of mannerisms similarly to a "tell" in Poker. They are behavioral clues coaches should be aware of that provide valuable insight into an athlete's actual mental state.

In order to detect changes in individual mannerisms it helps to know the athlete well. This includes how they conduct themselves when things are going just fine. When athletes don't act their usual selves, there is a reasonable chance they are experiencing negative thoughts or feelings. These negative thoughts and feelings make it harder to self-motivate if their heads are somewhere else other than completely in the game. I worked with one big league pitcher who had a tendency to touch his cap more often when he felt physically tired. To an outside observer, touching one's cap a few extra times in-between pitches may go unnoticed. However, as someone who knew this athlete well it was apparent he was experiencing some type of discomfort. When I highlighted how he touched his cap more often during the later innings, he acknowledged doing so anytime he felt physically exhausted. He was able to improve awareness into his tired clue, and used self-motivation to muster up just enough energy and will-power to get him through the final inning in his next start.

Another athlete I worked with would avoid eye contact with teammates after making an in-game error. In her case, she would spend the next five or ten minutes preoccupied with self-disappointment instead of continuing with full gusto. A third athlete would become silent around teammates in the locker room at halftime if he played poorly in the first half. His self-pity would spillover into the start of the second half where his performance was predictably impaired. For each of these athletes, changes in mannerisms were uncharacteristic and were improved using self-motivation to reassert feelings of optimism.

Critical Skill #8: Passion for the Game
When we listen to interviews of Hall-of-Fame athletes in all the major sports we will notice a universal theme among all of them: they love their sport! When we are truly passionate about something we are eager to dedicate and commit ourselves to that passion without hesitation. A true love of the game is an energetic attribute careered athletes share because they are always inspired to compete and never want to stop. Just ask MLB Hall of Famer Willie Mays who famously repeated "Let's play two!" He loved baseball so much that one game a day was not enough for him. His love of baseball contributed to Mays' amazing career.

There are instances when athletes are not as passionate about their sport. In these cases there is the potential for workable solutions to re-spark their interest. To better understand their situation, questions we may ask include when they started feeling less interested, and what is contributing to their diminished interest. As we assess for passion for the game it's important to keep in mind that a lack of passion is only significant if it is causing performance issues on the field. Some athletes may be more apathetic about their sport but continue to be successful. But when athletes show disinterest, and their disinterest is clearly affecting their performance, this becomes an issue we need to address.

Burnout is a great example when athletes start losing their passion for a sport. In these instances athletes tend to view their sport more as a burden rather than as a source of enjoyment. When burnout happens, athletes start casting their sport in a negative light. Their negative thoughts towards their sport begin outweighing the benefits, causing a diminished desire and passion to compete.

To illustrate burnout, I worked with one professional baseball player who felt the pressure to compete was no longer fun. As we discussed his burnout further, we soon discovered the root of his diminished interest was triggered by his father who was living vicariously through him. This added anxiety caused him to overlook aspects of baseball he continued to enjoy. To resolve the situation we formulated a plan that was within the athlete's comfort zone. We began redirecting his focus back onto the positive aspects of the game which he continued to enjoy. Eventually, he communicated the added pressure directly to his father who was receptive and began backing off

Critical Skill #9: Ability to Focus

The ability to focus is a necessary mental skill every athlete should master. Strong focus minimizes unnecessary thinking and distractions so athletes can maximize execution of their physical mechanics. When athletes are 100% focused they sometimes resemble robots: they go through the programmed motions exactly as planned. An example of an athlete who embodies powerful focus is NFL Quarterback Tom Brady. When Brady performs you could see the strategic calculations based on his eye movements as he scans the field before each snap. In Brady's case, it is visibly obvious his head is completely in the game focused on reading the line and executing the play.

Maintaining consistent focus can be a challenge for many athletes. The majority of athletes will experience focusing difficulties at least at some point in their careers. The fewer these instances the better. When athletes struggle with focus more frequently, this presents a greater cause for concern. A loss of focus can be caused by many factors including: on-field distractions; off-field distractions; negative feelings; negative self-talk; negative memories; a lack in confidence; or difficulty self-motivating. As we assess for focusing skills we want to learn when athletes are most vulnerable to losing their focus. This way we can work together to prevent a similar repeat in the future.

In the sports world strong focusing capabilities are often referred to as "the zone" or "the flow" (they are the same thing). All of us have experienced the zone multiple times in our lives. Have you ever read a great book, become immersed in playing video games, watched a great movie, or driven long distances? These are common time when we go into the zone only to realize hours have flashed by without us realizing it. When we enter the zone our brain waves slow down to the Alpha state as we become immersed in the moment. Athletes who are committed to practicing our strategies, by making them a part of their automatic routines, are significantly more likely to eventually find their flow. To improve an athlete's focus quicker I strongly recommend incorporating Focusing Band-Aid strategies as soon as possible.

Critical Skill #10: Personal Goal Setting
Nearly every large corporation sets goals prior to each fiscal year, including setting expectations for quotas, productivity, profits, and growth. Goal setting is also a valuable tool athletes can utilize to maintain determination and focus. Goal setting is similar to keeping your eye on the prize; it gives athletes something to strive towards and to reach for. When athletes set specific goals for themselves, they are more likely to work harder because they have a specific ambition in mind. Personal goals can be either short-term or long-term, and they may target an array of desired accomplishments including: statistics; win record; preparation and approach strategies; or a promotion within the sports ranks. Because there are several recommended guidelines as we explore goals, we will discuss goal setting further in chapter two.

CHAPTER 2

Session 2: Building a Road Map

Question: How do you eat an elephant?
Answer: One bite at a time.

Overview of Session Two

If someone told you to eat an entire elephant, you would probably stare at that person thinking to yourself how is that even possible. Aside from not wanting to eat an elephant anyway you would have a tremendous task ahead of you that would take time. To help athletes build all-around mental toughness that will endure throughout their careers, we have to take a gradual approach by taking one step at a time. Rushing their progress may have temporary benefits, although doing so may not get to the core of a problem. In addition, it may not give athletes enough time to learn important skills if we hastily rush them out the door.

Contrary to popular layman's perception, no sports psychologist has a magic formula to solve every athlete's problem in a single day. If this were the case word would spread fast and there'd be no need for sports psychologists. In reality, the mental game takes time to develop. Rather than applying quick-fix solutions and then sending athletes along their way, we will be taking a prudent approach to ensure athletes truly benefit.

If you are not a SPET coach, you can skip to the "Education" section of this chapter. For SPET coaches, the purpose of session two is to establish a roadmap depending on what we want to accomplish. This will set the tone for future sessions as we begin introducing powerful new tools athletes can start using now. In session two we will cover five topics:

1) Review our Findings
2) Introduction to SPET
3) Education
4) Goal Setting
5) Predicting Performance

1: Review our Findings

The start of the second session is a great time to review what we have discovered since the assessment interview. Time in between meetings allows us to process all the information we have collected so we can formulate additional questions we may want to ask. The purpose of the review is to: summarizing our findings while it is still fresh in both our minds (the coach and the athlete); to confirm identified critical mental strengths and critical mental areas for improvement; and to explore any additional insights athletes may have come up with over the past week. In many cases, the assessment interview will have enabled athletes to think more critically about themselves and make new personal discoveries. Any additional information can be taken into consideration as we continue.

2: Introduction to SPET

An introduction to SPET is important for those using this model from beginning-to-end. Once we have assessed and determined what is impacting performance, an introduction to SPET prepares athletes for what lies ahead. Athletes who understand the SPET process, including how the model is designed to help, are more likely to commit themselves to practicing the strategies taught to them. The techniques we will use are based on the principle that each strategy will prepare them for the next. We are starting with simpler techniques that will help transition them as they learn more advanced techniques each week thereafter. Using this "building blocks" analogy can be useful to illustrate the importance of practicing each technique on its own. Their commitment to practicing these techniques will determine their rate of progress. Before they can relearn to swim, they need to learn how to retread water first. The quicker they can learn to retread water, the quicker they can relearn to swim.

Many athletes appreciate a review of the stages of SPET so they can begin understanding how the model works. This involves briefing them about the content of session two; followed by learning relaxation skills in session three; improving positive thinking patterns in session four; integration of a relaxed body and a calm mind (aka all-around poise) in session five; and imagery training in sessions six and seven. Reviewing these steps demonstrates we have a specific plan of action, and that our plan of action will produce real results.

3: Education

As a clinician, offering psycho-education regarding mental health disorders and associated symptoms is a powerful way to help patients begin rationalizing their illness. Knowledge is in fact power. Helping them understand why they feel the way they do (without overwhelming them with too much information) often provides an immediate degree of comfort knowing they're not alone and that there are treatments out there. The same applies to working with athletes. Normalizing mental performance issues through education can equally provide much needed relief while instilling hope; hope they can improve. It's important for athletes to remember that despite their talents, they are still human. Fast or slow, strong or weak, tall or short, nature doesn't discriminate based on one's physical potential. Athletes are equally prone to mental breakdown under the wrong set of circumstances. Their adversities just happen to revolve around athletic performance.

Since athletes are no more immune to mental performance issues compared to other walks of life, it may help to explore their expectations of themselves. Do they accept the fact that they are vulnerable just like everyone else, or do they consider their mental performance issues to be unacceptable because they happen to be tremendously gifted in sports? One important distinction which separates professional athletes from others is they have the additional pressure of being in the spotlight. This is a valid factor we should consider. When others are watching us, struggling with mental performance issues can draw a lot of negative attention and be a very lonely experience. As we remind athletes they are capable of change, we want them to relax a bit so they can feel more optimistic. A renewed sense of hope can re-spark their motivation so they may clean the slate and give it their best effort.

There is great value in educating athletes regarding the relationship between cause and effect. An example of this is in my work with "Blake." During my assessment of Blake, he explained how five minutes prior to each game he would throw up (the effect) due to feeling overly nervous (the cause). Blake went on to describe when he threw up, everybody, including fans, teammates, and opposing players, would gawk at him and make disgusted faces. As a result, Blake was slow at finding his groove once the game started. Naturally he felt embarrassed, ashamed, and obsessed over thoughts of "what is wrong with me?"

Blake and I started off by reviewing education about the links between anxiety and vomiting to normalize what was happening to him before games. As I reviewed how relaxation, positive thinking, and focusing skills could be combined to address his issue, I witnessed a fleeting smile run across his face. For Blake, he really needed to hear there was hope and that he wasn't the "freak" which he made himself out to be. Almost immediately we began incorporating relevant techniques into his routine which he could test out on the field. Over the next several weeks, Blake committed to practicing these techniques multiple times each day. After four weeks since our initial session, Blake's vomiting before games completely went away.

4: Goal Setting

Overview of Goal Setting
Establishing individual goals for SPET will become a major focus of our work after the assessment interview. Regardless of your role with athletes, teaching them to set personal goals is a fantastic way to keep them motivated and inspired throughout the season. In regards to SPET, creating goals serves three purposes. The first purpose is to teach athletes how to establish appropriate goals, including how to set *realistic* goals on their own. Second, goal setting can serve as a monitoring tool to measure an athlete's rate of mental performance progress during SPET. We will use session two as our benchmark to compare progress each subsequent session. The third purpose of goal setting is for us to monitor the effectiveness of the strategies we are incorporating. When athletes show continued improvement towards their goals, we may continue with the stages of SPET. However, if athletes are having a hard time reaching their goals, we may need to explore what is impeding their progress and adjust our approach (such as creating or implementing new Band-Aids). Progress towards goals should be monitored at the start of each session in case there is goal stagnation so we can address it immediately.

Recommended Guidelines for Goal Setting
In my experience, athletes who set short-term and long-term goals for themselves tend to experience greater success as a whole, compared to athletes who simply show up to the field every day. Regardless of your role with athletes, you should seriously consider talking to athletes about setting their own personal goals. While collaborating on goals there are several recommended guidelines to follow. The first is to limit the number of goals to either one or two. This makes it easier for athletes to remember their goals and strive towards them. When athletes have more than two goals they tend to eventually dump a goal. Creating goals and abandoning them is a bad habit to get into. If athletes get into habits where they regularly create and scrap

goals, it may affect their morale over the long term, especially if they scrap goals due to progress stagnation.

A second recommendation for goal setting is changing or adjusting goals over time as needed. Flexibility is important because some athletes may find themselves in an unexpected predicament where achieving original goals becomes more difficult than previously expected. When athletes fall too far behind, or experience unanticipated circumstances, modifying goals will be important. Modifying goals ensures athletes have something to strive towards at all times. Adjusting goals not only teaches athletes how to modify goals independently, it teaches them they can do so while maintaining feelings of optimism.

A common scenario when modifying goals should be considered is when athletes are slower at developing certain mental skills. Every athlete will develop mental skills at their own rate. However, for those athletes who need more time, current struggles on the field may make it impossible to achieve initial goals. For example, if an athlete has a horrendous first half of a season, where achieving an original goal becomes seemingly impossible, this would be a good time to reformulate new goals focused on the second half of the season. By reformulating goals under these circumstances, athletes can put the recent past behind them and direct their focus onto the future.

The fourth recommendation of goal setting is using *SMART* guidelines. SMART is an acronym for: Specific; Measurable; Attainable; Realistic; and Treatable. When goals are SMART, we can fulfill each of the three purposes of goal setting discussed. Let's review the acronym:

Specific:
Specific goals are goals that are clearly defined. Specific goals hone in upon specific aspects of an athlete's game they want to improve. Examples of specific goals would include: to make a positive thought in between each inning in baseball; to use positive imagery before every free throw; or to use a specific focusing technique before each snap in football. These examples clearly dictate what an athlete needs to do to improve mental soundness. These

goals clearly illustrate where and when an athlete needs to start using certain mental enhancement tools.

Goals that are unspecific are vague in their wording. Contrary to the specific goals we just offered, unspecific versions of these goals would include: to think more positively during games; to increase positive imagery; and to focus better. Okay, great. While these goals have the right intentions, athletes would not have a clear roadmap of what they need to do to reach their goals and improve their mental game. Instead, we want to define goals in a way they know exactly what they need to do to improve.

Measurable:
Measurable goals are goals we can tally-up or count. They involve numbers in the wording of the goal to measure progress by. By taking a benchmark frequency of where they stand now during session two (think of it as taking a "snapshot" into their current situation), we can compare this benchmark to later sessions, thereby measuring their extent of progress. Measurable goals can include frequency or percentages. Examples of measurable goals may include: using positive imagery before every free throw (100% of the time); rush for 1000 yards in a season; make 75% of field goals; use deep breathing before each serve (100% of the time); or reach a batting average of .300 in baseball. So say an athlete has never used positive imagery before a free throw but wants to start using positive imagery every time. Their goal may be to use positive imagery from 0% of the time to 100% of the time before each free throw. Or a field goal kicker may say: improve field goal rates from 60% to 75%. Or a pitcher's goal may be to: think a confident thought before each pitch from 20% of the time to 100% of the time. Other options for goals may include: get on base twice per game; rush for 100 yards the next game; run a mile in under five minutes; bench press 200 pounds, etc. These are just some examples you may consider.

Attainable:
Attainable goals are goals that an athlete has the potential to achieve. This means that despite their physical size, speed, strength, or any other physical

characteristics, believing they can achieve their goal is probable. For example, in basketball it may be attainable for many athletes to score 10 points in a game. But, if that athlete only gets five minutes of playing time each game, scoring 10 points is probably out of their reach. Additionally, we're probably not going to ask a baseball player who lacks size and power to suddenly hit a lot of homeruns. As we consider goals we want to set goals that are within the realm of possibility for that individual athlete.

Realistic:
Realistic goals are fairly self-explanatory and are similar to attainable goals. Realistic goals are goals that athletes in general have the potential to achieve. For example, while elite Major League baseball players may set goals to hit .300 in a season, setting goals to hit .400 is probably unrealistic given that no one at the MLB level has hit .400 since Ted Williams in 1941. In this case, despite one's talent and potentials setting expectations that are too high may set them up for failure. In establishing goals that are realistic athletes will have realistic aspirations to strive towards.

Treatable:
Treatable goals are goals that can be improved through our work with athletes. This means as we work to build critical mental skills and teach them our strategies, we may reasonably expect to have a positive impact on them.

Non-treatable goals are goals that involve factors completely out of our control. Non-treatable goals are situations when an athlete's fate is left up to the decision of others. Examples of non-treatable goals would include: increased playing time; starting for a team; or to get drafted. Although these goals may be realistic for some athletes, these decisions are ultimately decided by coaches, team staff, and scouts. Further, these goals have nothing to do specifically related to on-field performance. Therefore, we may want to avoid these goals since we have little authority and control over these decisions.

Once we have collaborated on goals, it helps for athletes to write them down on a piece of paper and take them home as they leave. A handful of athletes will forget their goals if they don't have a hard copy to remind them. We want to encourage athletes to keep their written goals in a safe place where they are easily accessible and away from the eyes of others to maintain privacy.

5: Predicting Game-Day Performance: Green Flags – Red Flags

What if I told you there was a way we could predict an athlete's performance on game day? And I don't mean by studying stat sheets, looking at recent hot streaks, or by comparing opponents on paper. Although it is obviously impossible to predict how an athlete will perform with 100% accuracy, there is a way to improve our odds. Many athletes experience pre-game themes that can spill into a game. Some of these themes are a boon for athletes (green flags). Other themes hint that an athlete is going to have a bad day (red flags).

Pre-game green flags indicate an athlete is more likely to play well that day. When we look at an athlete's pre-game and post-game history, these green flags typically precede a successful performance. Although green flags will vary among athletes, common pre-game green flags include: feeling positive; thinking positively; being in a good mood; acting one's usual self; feeling rested; having eaten a satisfying meal earlier in the day; enjoying the pre-game music over the loudspeaker; having a special person attend a game; mingling with teammates, and so on.

Perhaps the most infamous green flag is superstitions. Athletes often incorporate superstitions into their pre-game routines because for them superstitions represent a positive omen. Whether athletes eat the same meal on game-days (Red Sox Hall-of-Famer Wade Boggs had to eat chicken), put on their uniform the exact same way each time, or hop over the foul line as they reach the playing field, these athletes tend to correlate superstitions with success. Historically in their mind, their superstition represents a green flag.

Pre-game red flags are indications that an athlete may struggle that day. When we look at an athlete's performance history we may notice there were early warning signs signaling something was off. Common red flags include: negative feelings; thinking negatively; feeling moody; not having slept well; having other things on one's mind; a recent fight with a significant other;

feeling hungry; feeling hung over; or uncharacteristic changes in mannerisms. When athletes experience red flags prior to games, history would show athletes are more likely to struggle. In many cases these red flags may be subtle, yet indicate an athlete is not in the ideal mental state of mind to compete.

The purpose of identifying green flags and red flags is so athletes can begin manipulating pre-game routines to their advantage. By increasing the frequency of green flags, and by reducing the frequency of red flags, athletes have the opportunity to potentially improve their performance on game days. In some cases, manipulating flags will be easier. In other cases, we may have to use our creativity to find solutions.

One athlete I worked with reported a major red flag was when he isolated from teammates before games. Any time he did so, he usually ended up playing below his potential. His solution was to force himself to tell rehearsed jokes to teammates the next time. Another athlete reported when he felt tired prior to starts, he had a harder time focusing. His solution was to get a super comfortable pillow, wear earplugs, avoid alcohol, and go to bed earlier the night before starts. A third athlete reported when he had fights with his significant other, things usually didn't turn out so well on the field. His solution was to proactively avoid conflicts with his significant other 24-hours prior to games.

Identifying and monitoring flags is simple. There are two steps to the process. The first step is for athletes to create a log or journal where they can list the suspects on paper. Phone memos and tape recordings are also a great option because athletes can monitor their tone and vocal excitement levels prior to games. In many cases athletes are shocked when they go back and listen to old recordings. They either say "wow I spoke confidently that day," or, "my god, I was destined to fail."

The second step to monitoring flags is by noting how the athlete actually performed after the game. As athletes keep track over time, correlations and common themes typically emerge. This information is extremely valuable because the sooner they can identify their flags, the quicker they can manipulate flags to their advantage. Again, knowledge and information are power.

End of Session Two

At this time we may offer athletes homework to begin monitoring and tracking flags. When we meet athletes the next time (for session three if using SPET from beginning-to-end), we can use check-in to review their findings and start exploring ways to increase the frequency of green flags while reducing the frequency of red flags.

CHAPTER 3

Session 3: Stress Management and Coping Skills

"Courage is fear holding on a minute longer."
-GEORGE S. PATTON

Overview of Session Three

Fear is uncomfortable. We don't enjoy experiencing fear. When we are threatened our autonomic nervous system kicks in, causing a fight, flight-or freeze response. The role of the sympathetic nervous system is to regulate our organs as it keeps our heart ticking and lungs pumping without us having to think about it. Stress can have similar effects on our bodies. When athletes feel stress the body releases hormones that instigate uncomfortable physical reactions. When stress reduces performance we refer to it as "performance anxiety." Athletes who can manage stress symptoms, by postponing stress a little longer, are more likely to maintain control over their finely tuned mechanics. Relaxation skills are counter strategies to physical stress symptoms. When our body feels relaxed, it's easier for us to perform to our potential.

Relaxation and coping skills are the ABC's of SPET training. These are simple, basic tools athletes can use to improve stress tolerance. Relaxation and coping skills target physiological stress symptoms (i.e. increased heart rate, blood pressure, sweating, tightening of muscles, etc.). Once athletes learn to keep stress symptoms in check, they will build other critical mental skills quicker. Relaxation and coping skills are the next step. Unless you are a SPET Coach, you may jump directly to the "Mindfulness" section of this chapter. SPET coaches will want to continue reading so they may start session three with check-in.

As the Start of Session Three

1) Ask about progress towards goals; adjust and modify goals as needed
2) Review pre-game green flags and red flags; explore new discoveries; explore ways to increase the frequency of green flags; explore ways to reduce the frequency of red flags
3) Find out if the athlete currently uses any relaxation or coping strategies, or has in the past
4) Consider using Band-Aid strategies as needed to target specific critical mental skills

At the start of session three we can begin by asking athletes about their progress towards goals. Although expecting progress this early on may be premature, sometimes their responses will surprise us. While many athletes will deny progress, a handful will report they started making immediate changes to their game because they felt inspired. This shows commitment and problem solving skills. Other athletes may not yet know what changes they need to make. This should be anticipated because it is our job to teach them.

If we assigned homework (to begin tracking green flags and red flags), we may begin by reviewing their findings. This involves going over their journals or logs to seek out any patterns or trends. If we identify any patterns we can begin exploring ways to increase the frequency of green flags and reduce the frequency of red flags. If no flags were discovered athletes should be encouraged to continue tracking flags the following week. In cases when athletes failed to search for flags during the week, we want to stress how important flag identification is for them. Additionally, we must stress the importance of follow-through on homework assignments so we may squash potential bad habits in the bud before they become habitual. Athletes who do their homework on a weekly basis will show significant progress each week. Those who don't will come back the following week with the same problems.

Before we introduce relaxation skills, we can learn a lot by asking whether athletes currently use or are aware of certain relaxation techniques. This lets us know where the athlete currently stands, and it gives us an idea into their immediate need to learn these skills. Athletes who already use relaxation strategies are generally one step ahead because they have tools to calm their bodies. Athletes who don't use relaxation strategies will need to spend more time mastering these skills before moving on.

At this time we may consider incorporating Band-Aid strategies to target specific critical mental skills. Whether we are adding Band-Aids to solidify a mental skill, or using them to address an urgent issue, Band-Aids can be implemented at any time.

Content of Session Three

1: **Mindfulness**
2: **Deep Breathing**
3: **Muscle Relaxation**
4: **Grounding**
5: **Guided Meditation**

1: Mindfulness:

Overview of Mindfulness
In today's world, the countless distractions we encounter every day makes it harder than ever for us to maintain self-awareness of our mind and body.

With all our fancy gadgets and technologies, along with our busy lifestyles, we are more likely to lose touch not only with our surroundings, but within ourselves. In many cases we become so preoccupied with our smart phones and computers that we neglect important awareness into how we are thinking and feeling at any given moment. This can turn into a problem if athletes are unaware their physical or mental state represents a problem that needs to be addressed. Athletes who more cognizant of their physical and mental states tend to be quicker at making the necessary adjustments needed to resolve their situation.

Mindfulness exercises are a warm-up to get the athlete's neurons firing. They help stimulate important areas of the brain in order to improve self-awareness. Research shows mindfulness can promote emotional regulation, including our ability to control when we feel anger or stress. The better athletes are at recognizing a negative feeling, thought, or physical symptom, the quicker they can take action. Additionally, mindfulness is an effective tool to help athletes build focus while tuning out distractions.

Think of mindfulness as a "here-and-now" experience, where people redirect all of their attention onto the present moment. We are starting with mindfulness because it will prime athletes for upcoming relaxation strategies. We are getting the athlete's "feet wet." Although there are many ways to practice mindfulness, I use the "Bubblegum Mindfulness Exercise." This exercise is a great way to help athletes "take a deep hard look inside" so they can improve self-awareness and identification of early warning signs.

The Bubblegum Mindfulness Exercise

The Bubblegum exercise is an off-shoot of a similar mindfulness exercise which uses raisins instead. I use bubblegum because in many sports athletes can chew gum while they compete. By using gum, athletes will experience chewing in a completely new way, thereby expanding their awareness and perspective during the experiment. For this exercise you don't have to choose gum, but I will use gum as an example to illustrate how a food item may be used to practice mindfulness with athletes.

The bubblegum exercise begins with the athlete putting a piece of gum into their mouth, onto their tongue. At first the athlete doesn't chew the gum, and instead is asked to pay close attention to the way the gum feels like in its dry state. During this time we can ask simple questions, including: what is the texture of the gum? What does the gum taste like before chewing it? How does the gum feel when pressed upon the roof of the mouth? And how do you visualize the piece of gum looking like sitting on your tongue?

Next, the athlete takes one bite into the gum as we ask them to describe the next stage of the chewing process. As they describe changing textures, flavors, and new physical sensations, the experience may begin to feel a little weird or uncomfortable. If this happens we want to validate that the experience can feel awkward. Yet, we want to encourage them to continue playing along since this exercise is a fantastic primer for upcoming performance enhancement strategies. We want them to step out of their comfort zone for a moment as they are stimulating commonly neglected regions in the brain. We want them to describe how the juices continue to develop, including how they salivate in reaction to the gum. This works to improve inner self-awareness of their physical bodies, so later on down the road they can spot stress quicker and then do something about it. Mindfulness is also a potent tool athletes can use on the field to tune-out unnecessary distractions, including auditory noises and over thinking. For example, an athlete can use the bubblegum mindfulness exercise on the field to redirect their attention if a crowd gets hostile during a pivotal moment in the game.

After describing their first bite athletes can start taking slow, purposeful bites into the gum. After each bite, athletes should continue describing any new observations they discover with as much detail as possible. The more detail they provide, the more they are demonstrating self-awareness and concentration. We can continually ask them to identify new aspects of the chewing experience they would have otherwise overlooked. After about five minutes of methodical chewing and questioning, the athlete can eventually spit the gum out, and talk about any lingering sensations or aftertastes to finish the exercise.

Once the exercise is over, athletes can describe their overall thoughts of the experience. Some athletes will report the experience was interesting and gave them a new perspective on how to think differently. Others will say it was out of their comfort zone. Either way, the uniqueness of this experiment should have a lasting impression on athletes so they can remember to be more mindful of themselves on the field.

2: Deep Breathing

Background
Deep breathing is the most common way for us to calm our bodies down when we feel stress. It allows us to take in vital oxygen and release un-nourishing carbon dioxide. The more efficiently we breath, the easier it is for valuable oxygen to travel throughout our body, including to our brain. Why not take advantage of air? Air is free. When we breathe correctly we can slow our heart rate, lower our blood pressure, reduce sweating, regain control over important muscle movements, and direct our attention to the task at hand.

When we get nervous our breathing patterns tend to change. Whether speaking in public, at a job interview, or when the game is on the line, stress has a nasty tendency to make us breathe the wrong way. If left unchecked, people who get nervous tend to take shorter, quicker breathes that actually reduces the amount of oxygen to our blood stream. This is why people end up feeling a fast pounding heart, sweating, lightheadedness, stomach knotting, and mental cloudiness when they get nervous. The heart is desperately trying to pump more oxygen throughout the body, including to the limbs and the brain. Fortunately, deep breathing can help to reduce these uncomfortable stress symptoms.

When most people breathe, they often do not use their entire lung capacity. Many of us have a lot of accumulated stagnant air just waiting to be exhaled. Deep breathing works to replace this stagnant air with fresh air. In teaching athletes how to maximize deep breathing efficiency, we can help them regain more control over their body when they feel stress on the field.

How to Apply Deep Breathing

Before we practice deep breathing we may ask athletes to model for us what they think deep breathing looks like. This lets us gauge to what degree they need improvement, including any modifications needed to improve breathing efficiency. When athletes show us proper techniques we can run through deep breathing a little quicker. When athletes misapply the technique, we may want to model the skill for them before practicing it together.

As we practice proper deep breathing we want to posture our bodies in a comfortable and upright position to open up our airways. This can be done either standing up or sitting down. Next, we place one hand on our stomach near the belly button, and the other hand on our chest above the heart. During each deep breath, we can follow the 5-2-4 mnemonic rule: We slowly inhale through our mouth for about five seconds until there is no more room for air; hold the breath for about two seconds; and then slowly exhale out the nose for about four seconds. Keep in mind that our exhale is equally important to our inhale. To test this theory out, take ten quick exhales in a row and see how you feel. You'll probably begin to notice lightheadedness. This is exactly what we hope to avoid.

As we take in each breath we should feel our belly and chest expanding at the same time. And as we exhale, we should feel our belly and chest retract inwards. After about three-to-five consecutive deep breaths we can take a brief pause, and then repeat the exercise depending on the athlete's progress. The first round of deep breathing practice is usually done together so athletes can watch us and replicate our technique. Subsequent rounds of deep breathing may be done together at the same time.

After Practicing Deep Breathing

Once athletes demonstrate correct deep breathing techniques on their own, we can start talking about when using the technique will be to their advantage. Ideally, athletes should use deep breathing throughout games to maintain some sort of consistency. The more they use deep breathing when they feel good, the less severe and quicker they can rebound when things suddenly become more stressful. Deep breathing becomes a preventative strategy in this regard. Equally important is for athletes to practice deep breathing during non-game situations. The more they can incorporate different strategies into their off-field routines, the more these strategies will become engrained into their on-field routines.

3: Muscle Relaxation

Muscle relaxation exercises are a great way to relax stressed-out muscles and to improve blood flow throughout the body. When athletes get nervous their muscles tend to tighten up, constricting veins and affecting blood flow. Have you ever watched a close tennis match and noticed how rallies seem to get longer as the situation becomes more intense? I was a competitive tennis player and I remember that feeling. This often occurs because as tennis players feel the urgency of a situation, even the slightest tension in muscles can make it harder to execute shots with precision. If muscles tighten up too much, athletes can physically succumb to the pressure. Muscle relaxation helps to loosen these muscles, and although not a miracle cure, will provide at least some relief. When muscle relaxation techniques are applied simultaneously with deep breathing, the advantages of these relaxation skills become even greater. Deep breathing along with muscle relaxation go together like peanut butter and jelly, or macaroni and cheese. Together they can potentiate (increase the potency) of the other.

Before practicing muscle relaxation techniques we want to identify which specific muscles tighten up when athletes feel stress or are nervous. Once we know exactly which muscles are vulnerable, we want to encourage athletes to keep these muscles loose throughout the game. By keeping these muscles loose when athletes feel emotionally relaxed, muscles shouldn't tighten-up as bad when stress shows it's ugly face. As with deep breathing, muscle relaxation serves as a preventative strategy in this regard.

Loosening muscles is simple. It can be done either by simply stretching muscles (like during warm-ups), or by tensing, holding, and then relaxing muscles. Other ways to relax muscles include using electronic stimulating technologies to return muscles back to homeostasis. Unfortunately, most athletes don't have this option during games.

As we work to relax specific muscles that are vulnerable to stress, it is generally good practice for athletes to keep all their muscles loose throughout their body and throughout the game. We can't always foresee if and when other muscles will be affected in the future. But we can teach athletes to remain proactive by taking additional preventative measures. We can do this by teaching athletes to use the "head-to-toe scan" technique. This entails starting by massaging their temples, and eventually moving on down to wiggling their toes. Areas of the body they can target during the head-to-toe technique could include: the temple; areas around the eyes; back of the head; jaw; neck; shoulders; upper back; middle back; lower back; sides; upper arms; forearms; wrists; hands; fingers; hips; rear; thighs; knee; calves; ankles; and feet.

4: Grounding

Background
Grounding is a tool to help athletes maintain composure when they anticipate feeling nervous on the field. Hey, if Russell Wilson of the NFL's Seattle Seahawks uses it, is must be good. Surely, he's not the only great athlete to use this technique. It really is effective. Grounding works to temporarily distract athletes away from stressful triggers on the field, by focusing onto something emotionally safer. It is called grounding because it mutes negative feelings, thoughts, and emotions; thereby allowing athletes to have greater control over the moment. Grounding is another form of mindfulness training. When athletes keep uncomfortable thoughts and emotions out of their heads, they will be in a better mental state of mind to compete. Remember that George S. Patton quote, "Courage is fear held on a minute longer?" Grounding allows athletes to postpone stress just long enough to get the job done.

During grounding, athletes will redirect their attention onto specific objects around the field as a source of distraction. By maintaining focus onto these objects, athletes can divert their internal attention onto something external (something tangible) and emotionally neutral. Athletes can choose nearly anything as their object of focus, including: billboards; banners; the scoreboard; marks on the playing field; lights; a blade of grass; water; a basketball hoop; diving board; field goal post, etc. As athletes gaze at these objects (for as long as they need depending on how much time they have), they want to focus all of their attention squarely onto that object. Because the effects of grounding within the clinical setting are so powerful, it is a popular go-to intervention for people who are experiencing panic attacks. So imagine, if grounding can help people overcome even the most agonizing emotional states, there is no reason why athletes wouldn't benefit from grounding as well.

How to Apply Grounding

I use a specific routine when I practice grounding with athletes. The exercise starts with deep breathing to calm their body, followed by muscle relaxation to loosen up their muscles (using a brief head-to-toe technique). Once athletes feel completely calm and relaxed I will ask them to quickly share any thoughts or feelings in that moment; thoughts and feelings which I will then ask them to proverbially throw out the window. It's not that I don't care about what they have to say. Rather, I want to use grounding to purge their minds so they can start practicing an important calming and focusing skill.

Grounding continues as athletes select one specific object within visual range. This object will become their "point of Zen," and will require all of their attention for the next five minutes. If you're in an office, objects to choose from can include: a clock; a scuff on the wall; a lamp; a picture or photo; a window; the ceiling, etc. Once an object is chosen, athletes are encouraged to begin describing that object in as much detail as possible while we as coaches remain mostly silent. In a sense, we want athletes to describe their chosen object as though they have a PhD in it, or as though they were the ones who designed it. They are the masters of that object and it is their job to describe it 100%. As athletes begin to struggle pointing out new observations, nine times out of 10 they will notice new features if we challenge them. This is the exact level of concentration we want athletes to replicate on the field when they use grounding.

After Grounding Exercises

Once grounding is over, we want athletes to provide feedback regarding the exercise. Many athletes express surprise by how much detail they noticed the more they stared at an object; details they previously neglected to recognize. For example, a scuff on the wall may begin to resemble a certain animal; a blade of grass may widen as it rises and has a serrated top; or the dial of a clock may have an arrow at the end of it. As athletes were transfixed onto an object, some of them will have experienced "the zone" or "the flow," even if only for a moment.

When athletes show acute focus during the grounding exercise we can start talking to them about when and how they can use grounding on the field. Grounding as a mental performance tool is more effective in stop-and-go sports. In sports such as football, tennis, golf, and baseball, regular pauses in-between plays give athletes more opportunities to use grounding. In sports with continuous action, such as in hockey, rugby, and soccer, opportunities to apply grounding are fewer. Fortunately, even in fast paced sports athletes can use grounding before games, during breaks, or during timeouts. So whether they stare into the eyes of a model on a corporate advertisement, or pay attention to the font and colors of a local business ad, all athletes can benefit from grounding to harness their focus and regroup.

One athlete I worked with would pick a cloud in the sky, stare at it, and then compare it to an animal or object. This all happened within a span of several seconds and helped him take a "mini vacation" away from the action so he could mentally reset. The more athletes practice grounding during non-game days, the less time they will need to effectively use the strategy on game days.

5: Guided Meditation

Background

Guided meditation is an imagery technique where we take athletes on a "mental journey." It involves us, the coach, to narrate a scenario which requires athletes to visualize, remain focused, and stay positive throughout the exercise. Guided imagery has additional benefits on top of improving focus: It requires athletes to continue incorporating relaxation skills into the exercise; It primes athletes for more advanced imagery techniques in session six (sensory-integrated-imagery-rehearsal); And guided meditation tests to what degree athletes can maintain a positive state of mind.

To test an athlete's ability to maintain a positive state of mind, I add a small negative twist during the narration. While the guided meditation experience will be mostly positive, there will be one exception. As I take athletes on a relaxing, feel-good journey, I will make one unexpected negative comment that seemingly comes out of nowhere. This element of surprise will test whether athletes can rebound from a negative moment, by preventing ensuing obsessive negative thinking patterns. Athletes who remained positive after the exercise will have passed the test and are ready for positive thinking practice in session four. On the other hand, athletes who were rattled by the negative comment may need to repeat the exercise by encouraging them to increase concentration onto the positive aspects of the experience.

How to Apply Guided Meditation

During guided meditation, we want to create a realistic imagery experience. We can accomplish this by using as much visual detail as possible. The more realistic we describe the situation, the easier it will be for athletes to concentrate and focus. As we walk them through each step of the scenario, athletes will remain silent the entire time. They will have the opportunity to share their thoughts and feedback after the exercise. The scenario we use should be something that is comforting to athletes. I typically use an ocean scene, because many people feel relaxed around water. Before proceeding, you may want to ask your athlete which scene they would prefer.

As we get started, athletes should be comfortably seated with their eyes closed. The exercise begins with a few deep breaths, followed by brief muscle relaxation to loosen their body. Once they are completely relaxed, we can proceed to describe the situation. Here is a sample script I typically use to give you an idea of how the exercise works. As I narrate my script, I always speak slowly, and take brief pauses in between sentences. This way, athletes can soak in the experience. Overall, the guided meditation exercise typically lasts between seven to ten minutes.

> Coach: *"As you take your deep breaths, you are beginning to feel relaxed, and in total control of your body. You are comfortably seated in your chair, with all your worries drifting out the window. As you sit here, you suddenly find yourself on a beautiful white sand beach, with nobody around. It's just you. There are no cars... there are no phones...there are no buildings...there are no children playing. All you hear is the gentle breeze, small waves crashing onto the sand, and the leaves of plants swaying back and forth in the wind. You are sitting in a lawn chair, on a patch of beautiful green grass, facing the ocean, inches away from the bright white sand. It is hot outside, but you are shaded by two tall palm trees on either side of you. You look up at the palm trees, and notice the sun beaming directly behind the leaves. You immediately look straight ahead, and stare out at the crystal blue water directly ahead of you. You can smell the salty air which is comforting. You begin to feel hot from the sun, when suddenly a bead of sweat slowly trickles down your forehead, onto your face, and onto your stomach. You notice that you're getting too hot, so you decide to cool down by going in the water. You know the water will feel just*

right. Not too hot. Not too cold. It will feel perfect. You slowly stand up, look straight ahead, and take your first step onto the sand. But the dry sand is hot from the blazing sun, so you quickly take a step with your other foot. Now the dry sand is burning your other foot as well. You start moving quicker towards the water. Step, after step. The sand feels like it is only getting hotter with each additional step you take. Finally, you reach the harder sand, where the waves just splashed over. It is wet and much cooler. Your feet don't sink into it. At that moment, a small ripple of water hits your feet. The water feels great. You have to continue towards the water to cool off. You enter the water, get in ankle deep...knee deep...waist deep...chest deep. Next thing you know, you are completely surrounded by water, except for your neck and head, which are poking out like a turtle getting some air. You look down in the water and see colorful fish swimming all around you. As you admire the beautiful fish...just then...you remember your last game where you stunk and felt ashamed about it **[this is the surprise negative comment]**. But you decide thinking about it won't help, so you turn around, face the beach, and gaze at the chair you were just sitting in moments ago. You notice your chair is still shaded by the two palm trees. You look up at the trees, and notice coconuts. You realize they are not palm trees, but they are in fact coconut trees! After gazing at the coconut trees for a few moments, you turn back around towards the ocean and see nothing but clear blue water. As you're staring off into the horizon, you notice a small island about 10 miles away. You start wondering what is on that island? And is anybody there? Now you are feeling cooled off, so you decide it's time to get out and back into your chair shaded by the two coconut trees. You slowly begin wading out of the water, eventually going from waist deep...to knee deep...to ankle deep. The next thing you know, you are completely out of the water and back onto the wet sand. Water is dripping off your body, and it felt great. It was not too hot...and not too cold. It felt exactly like you expected it would be: perfect! You begin taking steps towards your chair when you take that first step onto the dry sand. This time the dry sand doesn't feel as hot anymore because your feet are wet. However, it does start sticking to your feet. As you walk towards the grass, and out of the sand, you finally reach your chair. You slowly sit down, look up at the coconuts up above, and think to yourself, I feel great. [10 second pause] At this time, you realize you are no longer on a beach. You are sitting here with me. You are still taking deep breaths. And when you feel ready, open your eyes."

After Guided Imagery

After completing the guided imagery narration, getting the athlete's feedback regarding the experience is always interesting. Most athletes will tell us they felt relaxed and enjoyed the exercise. Others may have felt uncomfortable or had a harder time imagining. Regardless of their experience, I would estimate that over half of my athletes forget to mention the negative comment thrown out at them (where I reminded them that a previous performance "stunk"). In these cases athletes show an ability to maintain focus and a positive state of mind. Athletes who had a harder time concentrating, or were mentally thrown-off by my negative comment, may need to repeat the exercise until they learn to increase their focus onto the positive aspects of the exercise.

End of Session Three

At the end of session three we can review which techniques practiced during this session may benefit them the most. The more athletes begin incorporating newly learned relaxation techniques into their routines, the easier it will be to transition and learn new techniques that lie ahead.

At this time we want to make sure athletes start incorporating relaxation exercises into their routines. We may assign them homework to practice deep breathing, muscle relaxation, and grounding exercises multiple times daily both on and off the field. When we meet athletes the next time (in session four if using SPET from beginning-to-end), we will follow-up to ensure they are adding new skills into their repertoire.

CHAPTER 4

Session 4: Posititive Self-Talk and Positive Thinking

> *"You can't think and hit at the same time."*
> -YOGI BERRA

Overview of Session Four

Now that an athlete has improved control over their body using relaxation skills, the next step is to help them take control of their thoughts. The reason for practicing positive talk separately from relaxation skills is to ensure athletes spend enough time working to build each skill before introducing the next. Just as relaxation skills are used to calm the body, positive thinking is used to calm the mind. This will be important because as athletes improve relaxation and positive thinking skills, they will eventually work to integrate the two to build "all-around poise" in session five. If you are a SPET coach I suggest you continue reading. If you are not a SPET coach you may jump directly to "Thought Stopping" in this chapter.

Start of Session Four

1) Ask about progress towards goals; adjust and modify goals as needed

2) Review homework from session three: to practice deep breathing; muscle relaxation; and grounding daily
3) Review progress towards green flag and red flag identification; explore ways to increase the frequency of green flags, and reduce the frequency of red flags
4) Consider using Band-Aid strategies as needed

At the start of session four, we can begin by checking-in on progress towards goals. This helps us understand to what degree athletes are improving, including whether they are strengthening critical mental skills. Depending on their progress (or lack of progress) during session four, we may consider modifying or adjusting goals if needed.

We want to review homework from the previous week: to practice deep breathing, muscle relaxation, and grounding every day both on and off the field. Reviewing their homework gauges whether athletes are committed towards improving, and it helps us understand to what extent relaxation skills are helping thus far. If athletes successfully completed their homework they are ready to continue on with session four. If athletes didn't complete their homework, we may want to explore the barriers and review the importance of commitment.

Check-in is also the time to review green flags and red flags. We can discuss any new discoveries made and whether previous strategies to manipulate flags are working. If new flags were identified, we can continue solving ways to increase the frequency of green flags while reducing the frequency of red flags. If no new flags were identified, athletes should be encouraged to continue logging potential factors. If previous strategies to manipulate flags worked, we want to encourage athletes to continue using these strategies. If previous strategies to manipulate flags didn't work, we can always investigate new ways to tackle these flags.

Finally, we may consider incorporating Band-Aid strategies into session four if it will benefit our athlete's mental game. If athletes have any pressing needs that are hurting performance at this time, then we definitely want to consider using Band-Aids.

Content of Session Four

1: Thought Stopping
2: Positive Self-Talk and Positive Thinking
3: Flooding

1: Thought Stopping

Background

Have you ever gone to bed at night only to have trouble sleeping because you obsess over a negative event that happened to you earlier in the day? Perhaps you felt disrespected by a colleague or boss at work. Maybe someone cut you off in your car earlier in the day, or you had a fight with a significant other, or you cannot stop thinking about all the work you have to get done the next day. These are common negative thinking loops which are most prevalent at night, because as we go to sleep, we are alone with our thoughts. At night, there are fewer sensory distractions because when the lights go off there is less to see and less to hear. Yet sometimes, no matter how hard we try to think about something else, these negative memories keep creeping back into our heads like a broken record. Fortunately, thought stopping can break this unwanted cycle.

Thought stopping is a technique athletes can use when they find themselves having sports-related intrusive negative thoughts on the field. These negative thoughts may involve obsessing over a recent mistake, remaining upset over a bad call, or when athletes question their potential. If remained unchallenged, reoccurring negative thoughts can impede focus, reduce confidence, and make it harder to self-motivate. Thought stopping works to identify negative thoughts quicker so athletes can regain control and return to positive thinking patterns.

How to Apply Thought Stopping

I use a thought stopping technique that is simple to use, which I call the ABC's of thought stopping. ABC is an acronym for the three steps involved in thought stopping. They stand for: *Awareness*; *BAM it!*; and *Change it*.

1: Awareness
2: BAM it!
3: Change it

The first step of thought stopping, *awareness*, means learning to identify when a negative thought arises. Before we can change a negative thought into a positive thought, first we have to realize that a negative thought is happening. Since negative thoughts can arise abruptly, we want athletes to improve mindfulness of their thinking patterns during the mental skills building process. The quicker athletes realize they have a negative thought, the quicker they can change it into something more productive. Ideally, once athletes improve positive thinking patterns (by making them a part of their automatic routine), they will no longer have to use the same brain power to identify negative thoughts as they compete.

There are simple questions we can ask athletes to improve awareness of their negative thoughts. These questions include:

"Tell me some times in the past when you had a negative thought on the field, including: before a game; during a game; and after a game."

"Has a negative thought ever affected your performance?"

"What are some situations when you doubted yourself on the field?"

"Name some times when you had a hard time motivating yourself."

"Were there ever any times when you felt you would fail?"

"What are some examples when you struggled on the field, where it only got worse?"

Another way to improve awareness of negative thoughts is by offering hypothetical scenarios, to see if negative thinking patterns might arise. Sometimes these hypothetical situations will uncover the potential for negative thinking. This is especially true when athletes haven't yet experienced a certain situation in the past, but may become vulnerable if that situation arises. These hypothetical questions are a bit loaded and can expose the potential for negative thinking patterns. Examples of hypothetical questions we may ask include:

"What thoughts would cross your mind if you stunk the whole game but there was still some time left to play?"

"What would you be thinking if you were too tired and didn't want to play that day?"

"What would go through your mind entering into a crucial situation, when the game is on the line, and winning or losing rests entirely upon your shoulders?"

"How would you approach the next opportunity after a recent string of bad mistakes?"

"What would you be thinking after your team lost to a team you were supposed to dominate?"

"What would you feel after the game if an opponent who is weaker than you got lucky and beat you that day?"

The second step of thought stopping is to "*BAM it!*" *BAM it* is another way of saying "crush" that negative thought, metaphorically speaking. Although it is obviously impossible to literally crush a thought, BAMMING a negative thought means *visualizing* that you are crushing that thought. Athletes can do this by yelling "BAM" in their head. If shouting "BAM" in one's head sounds a little silly, I encourage this for a reason. Pretending to yell "BAM" provides athletes with a sense of empowerment and asserts control over their thoughts. Athletes may also stomp their foot or take a physical action to "BAM" a thought if that helps them.

The third step of ABC, *changing the thought*, means replacing a negative thought with a positive thought. Changing a negative thought into a positive thought can also take time to master. With practice, practice, practice, changing negative thoughts into positive thoughts will gradually become easier. According to Matthieu Ricard, a Buddhist Monk who is famously dubbed the "happiest man in the world," he believes that practicing making positive thinking 15 minutes a day will produce real results in as little as two weeks.

There are many ways to practice changing negative thoughts into positive thoughts. One of these methods is what I dubbed "*The Freud Game*" which will discuss next.

2: Positive Self-Talk and Positive Thinking

Background
This section talks about how to *change* negative thoughts once an athlete is *aware* of it and *BAMS* it. Negative thoughts can come in many different forms and are sometimes a little tricky to identify at first. Some thoughts are obviously negative. Others may have good intentions, but are worded in a negative way. For example, statements such as "I'm not sure if I can do this," and "my opponent is really good" express self-doubt. Statements such as "don't lose focus," or "don't let them intimidate you" mean well but are

negatively based. The more athletes can think thoughts that are completely positive, the better chance they have to remain hopeful and motivated. Therefore, words like "don't," "can't," and "won't" should always be avoided.

As we work to replace negative thoughts we want to make sure the new positive thoughts are *realistic*. Realistic thoughts mean that athletes can accomplish their positive statement. For example, if athletes tell themselves to "focus," we have every reason to believe that can actually happen. *Unrealistic* positive statements arise when statements are either impossible to achieve, or when expectations are too high. An example of an unrealistic thought would include a baseball player telling himself during a slump to "hit a homerun, hit a homerun." While hitting a homerun is possible, the statistical probability of actually doing so is not in their favor and thus sets them up for failure. In this case, realistic positive statements could be replaced by "see the ball, see the ball," or "hit the ball hard." These statements are much more likely to happen.

To start practicing replacing negative thoughts with realistic, positive thoughts, I created the "Freud Game." The Freud Game is really easy to use and you don't need to know anything about Sigmund Freud or psychology to benefit from it.

The Freud Game

One of the benefits of the Freud Game is it's an engaging way for athletes to practice changing negative thoughts into positive thoughts. It allows us as coaches to start by modeling how to do so, followed by the opportunity for athletes to apply what they learned from us. By showing them how to change thoughts first, it will be easier for them to do the same.

The Freud game is an interactive role-play where we take turns replacing negative thoughts with positive thoughts. Each round involves a back-and-forth dialogue. During each round, athletes and coaches will have multiple opportunities to respond to each other.

The role-play involves one person representing the athlete's negative self-talk side (the doubtful Super-Ego). The other side represents the athlete's positive self-talk side (the confident Ego). In a way we can think of the positive and negative self-talk sides as a devil on one shoulder and an angel on the other (like in the cartoons). The positive self-talk side, the angel, encourages the athlete to be positive. The negative self-talk side, the devil, encourages the athlete to think negative.

The role-plays begin with the coach playing the positive self-talk side and the athlete playing the negative self-talk side. The athlete starts off by making a recent negative statement, and the coach immediately responds by replacing that negative comment with a realistic, positive comment (this may require some quick wit by the coach to keep the exercise moving). The athlete then replies with a follow-up negative comment, and the coach re-responds with another positive comment. As the dialogue continues, each side will follow-up with four to five statements of rebuttal. As we continue to model how to make new positive statements, athletes will gain greater insight into what types of positive statements they can make.

After the round is over, the athlete and coach switch roles. This time, the coach becomes the negative self-talk side and the athlete becomes the positive self-talk side. The coach starts the new role-play by making a negative comment, and the athlete starts practicing to change that comment into a realistic, positive comment. After both sides rebut each other four or five more times, the athlete and coach can continue alternating roles.

At first athletes tend to have a hard time changing negative thoughts into positive thoughts. To help them, we may provide feedback on ways to do so in between role-plays. Through constant feedback and additional role-plays athletes will find it easier to change negative thoughts into positive thoughts as they go along with the exercise.

Once athletes learn to replace negative thoughts with positive thoughts without our help, they are finished with the exercise. If athletes continue to have a hard time they may need more practice. In general, I find that six to eight role plays in total is sufficient; meaning each of us played the positive self-talk side three to four times; and each of us played the negative self-talk side three to four times. If six to eight role-plays seem like overkill, I do it on purpose to hammer in the skill. On certain occasions, we may need to practice more than eight role-plays if their progress is slower. In other cases when athletes quickly catch on we may consider fewer role-plays.

Case Example of the Freud Game

To make sure it is clear how the role-plays work, here is a partial transcript of the technique being used on a baseball player. This example started with myself playing the athlete's positive self-talk side, and the athlete playing the role of negative self-talk.

> Baseball Player (negative self-talk): *"Don't strike out."*
> Coach (positive self-talk): *"Hit the ball hard."*
> Baseball Player (negative self-talk): *"I'm playing like crap today."*
> Coach (positive self-talk): *"This is a new opportunity."*
> Baseball Player (negative self-talk): *"This pitcher's stuff is too good today."*
> Coach (positive self-talk): *"See the ball. See the ball."*
> Baseball Player (negative self-talk): *"I can't hit his curveball."*
> Coach (positive self-talk): *"I feel ready. Bring it!"*
> Baseball Player (negative self-talk): *"Today's not my day."*
> Coach (positive self-talk): *"The day is not over yet. I'll make it my day."*

After modeling positive thinking for the athlete, we switched roles. This time, the athlete was the positive self-talk side, while I became the negative self-talk side.

> Coach (negative self-talk): *"I feel crappy today."*
> Athlete (positive self-talk): *"Uh...but my arm feels good today."*
> Coach (negative self-talk): *"But I had a bad pre-game."*
> Athlete (positive self-talk): *"Uh, uh...I won't let that affect how I play in the game."*
> Coach (negative self-talk): *"But in the past, a bad pre-game meant I would suck."*

Athlete (positive self-talk): *"But today's a new day."*
Coach (negative self-talk): *"But I'm not sure that today's my day."*
Athlete (positive self-talk): *"I'll make it my day and give it my best."*

After Practicing the Freud Game

As we mentioned earlier, it's natural for some athletes to initially struggle coming up with positive statements. This is totally acceptable. In the role-play example you may notice my athlete repeated similar positive statements to those I said earlier. This too is acceptable. By modeling positive statements for him he was better prepared to challenge his negative thinking patterns. Through additional role-plays, athletes will inevitably learn to identify completely new positive statements on their own. This is the goal. In the case of my athlete, it took him eight role-plays until he learned how to come up with his own unique positive statements.

As a final note, the Freud Game is a great exercise to practice as an entire team. This can be done by finding a willing volunteer; modeling the skill in front of the team; and then breaking the team up into pairs. By practicing in pairs, athletes can improve positive thinking skills just as effectively as they would if we sat down with them individually. Using a team format to practice the exercise can save you a lot of time and effort. When athletes can provide teammates with feedback on how they may improve, they will further hone their own positive thinking skills.

3: Flooding

Background

Like thought stopping, flooding is a strategy we can use on athletes to help them reduce negative thinking patterns. Flooding techniques are used to challenge worries, concerns, self-depreciating thoughts, and fears caused in anticipation that something bad might happen. For example, if a rookie is anticipating significant stress during their big cameo, flooding can be used to challenge their underlying concern. Flooding works to challenge negative thoughts so athletes have an "aha!" moment and realize how unproductive those thoughts are. By stopping negative thoughts before they get out of hand, athletes will have an easier time remaining positive, focused, and confident.

Although flooding is a common intervention to treat phobias and obsessive-compulsive disorders, I have tailored flooding specifically for athletes. My approach is way less intense compared to clinical flooding, and it doesn't threaten an athlete's ego. Flooding athletes involves taking current negative thoughts and instigating them to the point where their current negative thoughts start sounding ridiculous. As we bombard (flood) athletes with repeated negative follow-up statements, athletes tend to reformulate new perspectives, thereby enabling them to challenge an initial negative thought. Additionally, blowing their initial concerns out of proportion desensitizes them of their worries. If used correctly flooding is a tremendous gift to coaches and their athletes.

To keep the flooding experience light I incorporate humor into the routine. Adding humor ensures we don't "psych" athletes out and ensures we maintain a safe emotional environment where they can confront and challenge their fears. Adding humor is easy. We will use bizarre and absurd follow-up statements to highlight how counterproductive their worries are. Eventually, these worries will lose legitimacy. In addition, by pairing humor with worrying, athletes are being classically conditioned to view their worry more as laughable rather than as a valid concern.

Flooding can be used when athletes are apprehensive facing a certain opponent, are worried about embarrassing themselves, or anticipate something bad might happen. These are fear-based situations when athletes forecast a potential negative outcome even though it hasn't happened yet. For example, I overheard one coach mention that his star pitcher would rather walk a batter on a full-count than challenge the batter with a fastball and risk giving up a hit. This pitcher was probably sub-consciously concerned (fearful) about the emotional toll giving up a hit would have on his personal ego.

In his case, flooding probably could have done wonders on him. When left unresolved, fear-based thoughts impede progress because athletes are forced to work around their fears to find success. When working around these fears doesn't work either, failure can become a self-fulfilling prophecy. This doesn't have to happen. Unfortunately, it happens more than it should.

It's important to consider that not every athlete will need flooding. Some athletes know how to keep their concerns in check and know how to remain positive at all times. However, in situations where fear-based thoughts are interfering with performance, flooding is an excellent option to reframe their thinking.

How to Apply Flooding

To demonstrate how to apply flooding on athletes, the following is an excerpt of a flooding session I had with a collegiate softball player. This athlete was overly concerned that she would be benched because of a three-week long slump, leading to persistent stress and negative thinking patterns. The amount of self-imposed pressure was clearly hurting her performance, causing her body to tighten up, and causing her to overthink during each at-bat. It is always important to let athletes know beforehand when we will be flooding them (including how it works). This is to ensure they understand there is a method to our madness so they will play along.

> Coach: *"Imagine that you just struck out for the second time in a game. As you look over, you see your coach glaring over at you with those eyes of disappointment. How are you feeling?"*
> Athlete: *"I'm feeling horrible. I just know the coach is going to bench me."*
> Coach: *"That's a normal feeling to have when you've been struggling. But let's say that just as you take your first step towards the dugout, your coach immediately signals to you that you've been benched. How would you feel then?"*
> Athlete: *"I would feel really upset knowing I let my teammates down."*

Coach: "That's a terrible feeling. So you've just struck out for the second time in the game. You've just been benched. And you just let your teammates down. Now imagine that as you're standing near the plate, staring down at the ground in self-pity, a Pterodactyl (flying dinosaur) suddenly swoops over your head and craps all over you. How are you feeling then?"

Athlete: "Uh, I don't know [while giggling]. That's pretty weird. I would probably feel embarrassed."

Coach: "Yeah, that would be pretty embarrassing. So now you're standing near the plate. You've just struck out. You've been benched. You feel terrible. And a Pterodactyl just pooped on your head. As you're standing there, feeling all alone and even more embarrassed, you're covered in a ton of white dinosaur poop, which is slowly oozing down your jersey. And guess what? Suddenly, just then, your pants fall off. What do you think about that?"

Athlete: "Uh, that's weird too [while continuing to giggle]. I'm feeling even more embarrassed now I guess."

Coach: "But wait, there's more. You forgot to wear underwear! You've struck out, you've been benched, you're feeling terrible, you're covered in white dinosaur poop, your pants fell off, and you're standing there butt naked. Did I mention you were benched! What happened?"

Athlete: "Oh my god, that's pretty bad…can it get any worse?"

Coach: "It can! Because now every single fan in the stands, including your parents, are staring at you, laughing and pointing at the spectacle. I bet you want to just disappear, right? I mean, you've just been benched, and that's not even the worst part."

Athlete: "Oh no. This is horrible [while laughing]."

Coach: "Yup. And as you try and run towards the dugout to get away from it all, you suddenly trip and fall because your pants are locked up around your ankles. You've struck out, you've been benched, you feel terrible, you're covered in white dinosaur poop, your pants fell off, you forgot to wear underwear, everybody's laughing at you, and now

a tiger runs over to you, pees on you, and then bites your arm off. What are you thinking now?"
Athlete: "This is just too much. It keeps getting worse and worse. When will it stop?"
Coach: "It doesn't stop. Because all that time, all you were worried about was being benched. But you chose to worry. Was it worth it?
Athlete: "No, I guess it wasn't worth it."
Coach: "And now, your whole life is ruined. Because every time your teammates look you in the eye, they will laugh at you and no longer want to be around you. It all started because you were so worried about letting everyone down. You didn't think it could get any worse, but it did. Do you think you let them all down?"
Athlete: "Uh...no...not really. I gave it my best shot."
Coach: "How would you know if you gave it your best shot? You told me you were tensing up at the plate?"
Athlete: "Well I guess I could have worried less...and concentrated more on my approach instead of worrying about being benched."
Coach: "But you chose to worry about being benched, right? And because of that, the situation only got worse."
Athlete: "Yeah, but maybe next time I can do more to focus and relax."
Coach: "How could you possibly focus better the next time?"
Athlete: "I could probably focus more on myself and the situation instead of worrying about my coach. I guess all my worrying about being benched is not helping."

After Flooding

By flooding worries, fears, and concerns, many athletes start to challenge negative thoughts naturally. When athletes learn to extinguish negative themes, it only becomes easier over time. But if negative themes keep coming back, we may consider using flooding one-to-two times per week until athletes learn to control fears on their own. Flooding doesn't have to be done in person. It can be done over the phone, which is a great option when athletes are traveling on the road.

In the case of the softball player, flooding helped her realize she was spending too much time worrying about being benched and not enough time focusing on her approach. This was her "aha!" moment. I didn't even have to point it out. She had a cathartic revelation.

Humor also helped because after flooding, every time she worried about being benched she remembered a flying dinosaur pooping on her head. Her worry started becoming more of a nuisance rather than a concern. After two weeks of flooding, she worked hard to improve her approach on the field, and refocus onto what she needed to get done to compete. By the end of the season, she ranked third on her team in innings played.

End of Session Four

At this time we want to assign athletes with homework so they may begin incorporating positive thinking into their routine. This means practice positive self-talk on the field daily. When we meet with them the next time (in session five if you are a SPET coach), we can follow-up to see whether their positive thinking skills are improving.

CHAPTER 5

Session 5: Poise and Behavior Control

> "A man is but the product of his thoughts;
> what he thinks, he becomes."
> -MAHATMA GANDHI

Overview of Session Five

What we think, and how we feel, influences what we do. Now that athletes have practiced positive thinking to calm their mind, and relaxation skills to calm their body, they are ready to integrate the two to build *all-around poise*. Much like the peanut butter and jelly, or macaroni and cheese analogies, the mind-body connection can complement each other nicely by making the other stronger. On the other hand, they can also drag each other down. Distress in the body can deregulate the mind. And distress in the mind can deregulate the body. When we take control and sync the two together, they can unite into a single well-oiled machine. Session five will talk about this mind-body connection, including how to integrate the body and mind to establish all-around poise. For SPET coaches, you may continue reading on. For non-SPET coaches, you may skip to the "Poise Education" section of this chapter.

Start of Session Five

1) Ask about progress towards goals; adjust and modify goals as needed
2) Review homework from the previous week: to practice positive self-talk on the field daily
3) Check-in on green flags and red flags; explore solutions to increase the frequency of green flags, and reduce the frequency of red flags
4) Consider using Band-Aid strategies as needed

Per usual during check-in, we can start off by asking about progress towards goals. We can explore which mental enhancement strategies are helping, including to what extent. We want to ensure athletes are applying each of the strategies consistently and at the right times. When athletes show progress towards goals, we want to highlight their achievement to encourage a continued commitment towards utilizing recently learned strategies. If athletes show no progress, we may need to collaborate and adjust goals once we find out why goal stagnation is happening.

We want to follow-up with their homework from the past week: to practice positive self-talk on the field daily. If at this point we're unsure whether athletes have improved the skill, we can always do a quick role-play of the Freud Game to find out. Athletes who quickly change negative thoughts into realistic, positive thoughts are ready to move on. Athletes who need our help, or take longer to create positive thoughts will need a little more practice.

As we review green flags and red flags we can ask the standard questions: have any new discoveries been made over the past week? Have previous strategies to manipulate flags work? And what are some additional ways we can manipulate the frequency of flags? If no new flags were identified, we may encourage athletes to document potential flags for at least one more week just to be safe.

If there are any urgent performance issues, or when specific critical mental skills need immediate improvement, we want to incorporate Band-Aid strategies into session five. Even if there are no pressing issues, we can always take advantage of Band-Aids to give critical mental skills an additional boost.

Content of Session Five

1: Poise Education
2: Identifying Triggers
3: All-Around Poise Control

1: Poise Education

Poise describes our physical composure and body language. When we think of poise, we can think of being in full control of our body and movements. The goal of poise education is to teach athletes what to look out for when they are on the field. The better their awareness into their style of poise, the more proactive they can be to maintain a strong physical presence. Poise education includes reviewing both positive and negative signs of poise. Although we as coaches already have a good idea into what poise should look like, we want to ensure our athletes understand the same. Poise education is meant to help athletes think more critically about their own style of poise on the field in order to give them an ideal to strive towards: *all-around poise*. We will discuss what *all-around* poise is in a moment.

Positive Signs of Poise

Positive characteristics of poise are fairly obvious. The key term to consider when we talk about poise is physical "self-control." Self-control means discipline over the entire body, including eye and limb movements, subtle mannerisms, and calculated behaviors. When athletes look poised, their behavior is predictable because they are maintaining a strong degree of physical control at all times. Despite their highs or their lows, recent achievements or recent failures, their physical demeanor should be consistent when they demonstrate poise.

To understand how athletes perceive strong poise, we can ask them to name other athletes who exemplify poise. We may ask them to describe in detail what poise looks like in those athletes so we know they understand the concept. Most athletes do get it. For those who don't, learning strong poise characteristics is important so they may emulate these physical traits on the field.

Negative Signs of Poise

Negative poise indicates the body is unhappy. It signals the mind is upset in some form, causing their physical composure and demeanor to react accordingly. Athletes who act uncharacteristically may be showing signs of poise wearing down. Common warning signs include going through the motions quicker, increased fidgetiness, pacing, abnormal posturing, a defeated facial expression, and so on. We can tell when athletes are losing their poise when they act differently compared to when they appear relaxed and in good spirits.

Since negative body language is fueled by negative thoughts and emotions (the body is regulated by the mind's intentions), it can have a cyclical crippling effect back upon the mind. In turn, negative body language can instigate the upset mind further, making it harder for athletes to pick themselves back up. Here is a simple illustration to show this cyclical pattern of negative poise:

The mind is upset
↓
The body reacts and gestures it is upset
↓
Now both the mind and body are each upset
↓

The mind cannot help the body
⬇
The body cannot help the mind
⬇
The ship sinks

A huge red flag indicating all poise has been lost is when athletes react with exaggerated and excessive negative responses. These exaggerated and excessive responses typically include: slamming a bat against the water cooler; obsessing over a bad call by a referee or umpire; getting into verbal or physical fights; prolonged cursing; retaliation towards an opponent; or when athletes have a hard time being calmed down by teammates. These are over-reactions that indicate athletes have completely lost their cool and are not in mental control. If our athletes have engaged in these behaviors in the past, we need to seriously work with them to address their issues to avoid similar repeats in the future. In rare cases, it may help to refer athletes to anger management classes if their excessive responses are too consistent and common.

All-Around Poise

I have heard multiple coaches over the years tell athletes "poise" is one of the most important characteristics they can bring onto the field. Initially, I agreed. Yet as I continued working with athletes on an individual level, I quickly discovered that poise alone is not enough. Many athletes can fake poise in the short-term. But when the shit hits the fan over and over again, physical poise by itself is vulnerable to eventual breakdown. Physical poise is difficult to sustain when the mind is repeatedly bombarded with one bad result after another.

What coaches should tell athletes is *"all-around poise"* is the most important characteristic they could bring onto the field. I am more likely to agree with this statement. All-around poise necessitates full control over the mind *and* body as a single entity. Poise by itself has its benefits. But all-around poise is more holistic because physical poise is heavily influenced by an athlete's mental state. When there is harmony between a calm mind and a calm body, physical poise is much more likely to sustain under prolonged pressure. If the mind stays positive, the body is more likely to act accordingly. If the body acts calm, it's easier for the mind to stay positive.

An Example Highlighting the Importance of the Mind-Body Connection

A great way to help athletes reflect on the relationship between the mind-body connection is by offering the following comparison example. In this example athletes will clearly understand the links between the two:

> PITCHER A: "Pitcher A" pitches the ball, gives up a homerun, and then walks around the mound cursing under his breath, stomping his feet, while flailing his arms as the batter trots around the bases.

> PITCHER B: "Pitcher B" pitches the ball, gives up a homerun, walks around the mound, takes a deep breath, but does not react.

After proposing these two scenarios, the first question I ask athletes is which pitcher showed more physical poise. The answer is obvious, as athletes always know "Pitcher B" showed more poise. We can follow-up this question by asking them how "Pitcher B" showed poise, and how "Pitcher A" showed negative signs of poise. Again, answering these questions should be easy and allows athletes to see both ends of the poise spectrum.

The next question I ask is a bit trickier. This question is: which pitcher felt more upset, "Pitcher A," or "Pitcher B?" Perhaps unsurprisingly, many athletes respond that "Pitcher A" was more upset. This is sort of a trick question. Then my question to them is, how do they know "Pitcher A" was more upset? How do they know "Pitcher B" wasn't equally upset? Both of them gave up homeruns, so I would bet neither was happy with the outcome. This question becomes a source of discussion since we don't really know what each pitcher was actually thinking or feeling. Based on the limited information we do have, we know one pitcher maintained his poise while the other lost his composure.

The last question I ask is which pitcher is more likely to be mentally prepared to face the next batter? This question links the mind-body connection. Based on our understanding of all- around poise, including the cyclical relationship between physical poise and the mind, "Pitcher B" should be the answer. By maintaining his composure, "Pitcher B" should have an easier time to mentally regroup because in maintaining his physical poise he was exerting a greater degree of control over his actions. Whereas "Pitcher A" physically lost it, thereby having a steeper hill to climb to mentally rebound.

2: Knowing Our Triggers

Identifying poise-reducing triggers is an important component of SPET. At this stage, athletes should know how to remain positive minded while keeping a relaxed body. Now athletes are ready to begin integrating the two together at the same time to establish *all-around poise*. To foster all-around poise, athletes will simulate trigger situations that may otherwise threaten critical mental skills and physical composure. These simulations give athletes as many opportunities as they need to build mental resiliency using all their new tools via role-plays attempts. Through extended role-play practice, applying various strategies will gradually become automatic so athletes won't have to stop and think about what they need to do by the time they return to live competition. Once we identify their triggers, we will use the remainder of session five and all of session six to help athletes build resiliency to these triggers.

Triggers

When we think of triggers, we can think of triggers exactly like a trigger on a gun: when they are pulled, an explosion goes off. For athletes, triggers are specific situations on the field that set them off. Triggers impair critical mental skills, instigate physical stress responses in the body, and make athletes susceptible to losing all-around poise.

Most athletes will have triggers. Some will have more triggers than others. Examples of common triggers include: performing under pressure; immediately after a bad call by an umpire or referee; getting booed or heckled by opposing fans; after making an error or mistake; when they feel physically tired; or when athletes get one-upped by an opponent. Again, these are just some examples to illustrate triggers. To understand an athlete's unique triggers, including how their all-around poise may be impacted, we can ask the following four questions:

1: Which situations in the past triggered negative thoughts and feelings?
2: What were these negative thoughts and feelings?
3: Which situations in the past triggered physical stress and a loss in composure?
4: Where in your body did you notice physical changes?

Once we've asked these four questions, we will have identified their triggers and determined their trigger symptoms. With this information we are ready to begin building and solidifying an athlete's all-around poise.

3: All-around Poise Control Practice

All-around poise control practice simulates triggers so athletes can start practicing maintaining full physical and psychological control. It uses role-plays to give athletes unlimited opportunities to go through the actual physical motions while applying SPET strategies. This includes using relaxation skills to keep the body calm, positive self-talk to keep a positive mind, a heightened sense of awareness into their physical composure, and Band-Aid strategies to target critical mental skills.

As we recreate trigger situations during role-plays, we want to dialogue with athletes to monitor which steps they are taking to overcome the situation. Additionally, we want to continually offer vital feedback to improve each successive role-play attempt. Once athletes demonstrate they can effectively apply SPET tools without our help, they are ready to practice all-around poise control on their own.

To make the process of all-around poise control organized, here is an outline of the steps we can take:

1) Identify a trigger situation
2) Review which mental enhancement strategies athletes will use
3) Recreate trigger scenarios using descriptions to simulate a difficult situation
4) Observe how the athlete talks through and manages the trigger situation; provide feedback as needed
5) Repeat role-plays multiple times until athletes remember to apply SPET strategies without our help

Case Example

The following is an example of how I applied all-around poise control in the past. In this case we will use "Lisa" to illustrate the process:

> "Lisa" was the star soccer player on her college team. As the leading goal scorer, she experienced a lot of pressure to perform because she felt she was carrying the weight of the team on her shoulders. Being chosen as the team's primary penalty kicker put even more pressure on Lisa, because she was afraid of missing kicks and letting her teammates down. In practice, Lisa rarely missed penalty kick opportunities. But during actual games, she became overly nervous and missed over half her attempts.

The first step to helping Lisa was identifying her triggers. In her case the trigger was obvious: penalty kicks. Lisa reported that as she approached each penalty kick opportunity during games, her heart began to race, muscles in her legs would tighten up, she felt butterflies in her stomach, had a hard time concentrating, and was preoccupied with the fear of disappointing her teammates if she missed.

The second step of the process was to review which performance enhancement strategies Lisa could apply to improve her approach. This included taking deep breaths to calm her heart rate; stretching her legs to reduce muscle tension; positive self-talk to improve motivation and confidence; and positive imagery to improve focus (positive imagery will be discussed in chapter six).

As Lisa practiced all-around poise in front of me, she shared her thought process out loud. This allowed me to monitor whether she was going through the motions appropriately to manage her situation. In Lisa's case, she didn't need my feedback during role-plays because I could hear her problem solve commendably. Her monologue went like this:

> *"Ok. Here we go. I am about to attempt a penalty kick...what do I need to do first? Ok, I'm feeling nervous. I need to take deep breaths, and do some leg stretches. [she takes 3 deep breaths, and stretches out each leg] Ok, that feels better. My body feels good. What do I need to do now? I need to think positively! What am I thinking, what am I thinking? I'm thinking don't miss. Wait, I need to change that. I need to think positively. I can do this...I can make this shot. I will say to myself 'I've done this a million times in practice. I can do this again. I can do this.' My body feels relaxed. I feel confident. Now I need to focus. I'll take a few more breaths...maybe stretch out my legs again [she proceeds to take a few more deep breaths, and stretch out her legs again]. Ok, my body feels better. I know I can do this. What do I need to do next? Oh, I know. I will visualize taking a few shots in my head. I'm going to imagine each one going in the net [she simulates taking two penalty kicks]. Ok. I'm feeling pretty good. But I want to stay focused. I'm going to focus on a blade of grass...I'm going to stare at that blade of grass until I'm completely focused [she stares down at an imaginary blade of grass]. Ok. I'm ready. I feel focused and confident. Let's do this!"*

As Lisa continued to practice additional role-plays, her thought process became quicker and smoother. After four attempts with me present Lisa had rehearsed the steps enough times that she felt confident she could apply the skills on her own. Lisa committed herself to spending each day practicing all-around poise control, including on the field and in her room at night. Her dedication towards improving showed. Although her penalty kick rate only improved by 14% by the end of the season, by the end of the following season her penalty kick rate shot up to over 75%. Lisa stayed committed to using all her SPET strategies the entire time.

End of Session Five

At the end of session five we can assign homework for athletes to practice all-around poise control by simulating overcoming triggers on their own. This would include simulating trigger situations on the field during practice (which is highly recommended). And this could include all-around poise practice off the field, including while at home. Committing to this homework assignment will be important, as it will prepare them for *positive imagery* and *sensory-integrated-imagery-training* in session six.

CHAPTER 6

Session 6: The Imagery Experience

> *"You can't depend on your eyes when your imagination is out of focus."*
> -MARK TWAIN

Overview of Session Six

Session six integrates everything athletes have practiced thus far and takes it to the next level. Once athletes learn to maintain all-around poise control, they will be prepared for *positive imagery* and *sensory-integrated-imagery-training*. When athletes use these two visualization techniques they will be prepared to overcome nearly any difficult situation awaiting them in the future. The goal of positive imagery and sensory-integrated-imagery-training are twofold: it allows athlete to continue automating all the tools they have learned into their routines; and it prepares them for upcoming challenges they have yet to experience. At this time non-SPET coaches may jump directly into *"Positive Imagery"* of this chapter. SPET coaches should continue reading and proceed with the usual check-in.

At the Start of Session Six

1) Review progress towards goals
2) Ask about homework: to practice all-around poise control
3) Review green flags and red flags
4) Incorporate Band-Aid strategies as needed

At the start of session six we want to review continued progress towards goals. By now athletes should be close to their goals considering we would have previously modified or adjusted them as needed. If progress towards goals continues to stagnate, session six may be our last opportunity to amend them. As we discuss goals it may help to identify which SPET strategies are benefiting athletes the most, and which critical mental skills are the strongest. This way, athletes can be encouraged to continue relying on these skills as they work to implement new strategies to build other critical mental skills.

During check-in we also want to follow-up about recent homework: to practice all-around poise on and off the field. If we're unsure whether athletes improved the skill, we can run a quick role-play using their triggers to test how they may maintain all-around poise. If they show us which steps to use without hesitation, they are ready to move on. If they have a harder time doing so, we may practice a few additional rounds of all-around poise control until they get it down.

We also want to review green flags and red flags. This includes: discussing any new flag discoveries made over the past week; reviewing the effectiveness of previous flag interventions; and to continue exploring ways to increase green flags and reduce red flags.

Finally, we can consider using Band-Aids strategies as needed. Band-Aids could be used for any reason, including to solidify critical mental skills or when critical mental skills need a quick pick-me-up.

Content of Session Six

1: Positive Imagery
2: Sensory-Integrated-Imagery-Training

1: Positive Imagery

Positive imagery means visualizing a specific opportunity in the game and imagining being successful in that moment. For example, a pitcher may visualize hitting his target in the strike zone before an actual pitch. A competitive diver may imagine minimizing a splash. A field goal kicker may visualize feeling the football explode off his foot and directly through the goal posts. Or as with Lisa in the previous chapter, she imagined making her penalty kicks. Positive imagery is an easy skill to learn, yet offers tremendous benefits. These benefits include:

1) It lets athletes take "mental practice attempts" before taking real attempts
2) It allows athletes to focus exclusively on what they want to accomplish
3) It may increase the statistical odds of making actual attempts
4) Imagining a positive outcome promotes positive feelings and positive thoughts

A great example how positive imagery fulfills each of these benefits involves NBA basketball star Steve Nash. Nash reportedly visualized taking five to six free-throw attempts before each actual shot. This allowed him to mentally prepare and focus on what he wanted to accomplish (making the basket). The positive imagery technique was so powerful it surely contributed to his 90% career free-throw percentage, among the best in NBA history.

Before practicing positive imagery, there are certain factors athletes should consider. The first is knowing when athletes should apply the strategy. Depending on the sport, some athletes may have more opportunities to use positive imagery compared to others. In sports with continuous action (such as soccer, hockey, and rugby), athletes will have fewer opportunities to apply visualization techniques. In sports with pauses in between the action (baseball, tennis, golf, and football), athletes will have plenty of opportunities to use positive imagery.

A second factor to consider is knowing beforehand how much time an athlete has to use positive imagery during games. Whether athletes have five seconds or five minutes will determine how efficient they need to be with their time. The less time they have during pauses in the action, the quicker they have to apply the skill. While baseball players may have more time to use positive imagery in the on-deck circle, they will have less time to use the technique at the plate in between pitches. The quicker athletes learn to master positive imagery, the less time they will need to reap it's benefits.

A third factor to consider involves the addition of tactile objects into the positive imagery process (such as sports equipment). Tactile objects can trigger the brain into recognizing when something feels right (or wrong) so athletes know when they need to adjust and get more comfortable. Tactile objects can either be real (i.e. using an actual ball) or imagined (i.e. remembering the grip of a ball). Muscle memory in the brain is a very important concept in sports because when we hold an object and it feels right, it can trigger proper mechanics on how to handle a piece of sporting equipment. This is partially why athletes need preseasons to fine-tune their muscle memory and mechanics after a long offseason. If they don't use it, they might get a little rusty. The more we can take advantage of tactile senses during positive imagery, the more readily athletes can draw upon rehearsed visualizations later.

Returning to Steve Nash, part of his visualization approach involved paying attention to his grip of the basketball. If the ball felt awkward in his hands, he could take a moment to readjust his grip until he replicated exactly what it should feel like before a successful free throw. Other examples of tactile objects athletes may consider include: a pitcher finding the right grip on his curveball; the field goal kicker feeling the football explode off his foot; a swimmer recreating their rhythm as their arms torpedo through the water;

or a quarterback feeling the seams of the football roll off his finger tips to create that perfect spiral.

The fourth factor to consider before practicing positive imagery is to determine how the imagery experience will play out. We always want it to end on a positive note, but exactly how it ends can be left up to the athlete. For example, a tennis player may imagine smashing an ace by hitting their exact target. Or they may imagine jamming their opponent on a kick serve. Regardless of the positive outcome they choose, we want their imagined success to be realistic and achievable. We're not going to imagine a tennis player serving 150 miles-per-hour.

Case Example

Here is an example of positive imagery in action, using "Ben" as our example.

> "Ben" was a first-year Minor-League pitcher. Drafted straight out of high school, he had always relied on his 90 mile-per-hour fastball to dominate opponents. After getting drafted, Ben quickly realized that everyone could hit a 90 mile-per-hour-fastball at this level. This came as a shock to him because in high school no one could. Ben had good movement on his changeup and slider, but since he didn't have to rely on these pitches in the past, he didn't feel confident throwing them now. Each time his catcher signaled for a changeup or slider, Ben had no idea where his pitches were going. His coaches and teammates kept giving Ben advice on what he could do to improve, but none of these suggestions helped. He could tell others were losing confidence in him. But more importantly, he was losing confidence in himself. Prior to reaching out for help, Ben had walked a quarter of the batters he faced. His season had come to an end and he was worried that if next season he continued to struggle, he would be cut from the team.

As we take a look into Ben's situation, his primary mental performance issue was a lack of confidence in throwing the changeup and slider. Every time he would throw either of these two pitches, it turns out he would get little mini flashbacks of these pitches flying all over the place. These visions made him scared, hesitant, and caused him to tense up during each pitch. To break it down even further, Ben was using negative imagery by thinking about worst case scenarios. This led to a downward spiral of other critical mental skills, including reductions in stress tolerance, focus, and competitive spirit. Fortunately for Ben, positive imagery (along with a few other mental performance techniques) would be a godsend.

We began positive imagery by reviewing relaxation and positive thinking techniques. As Ben closed his eyes (with a baseball in hand) and imagined standing on the pitcher's mound, he admitted feeling doubtful he could throw a strike. He took three deep breaths in real life, followed by changing his negative thought ("don't over throw the catcher") into positive thought ("concentrate on your target") out loud. As Ben took his time to ensure he felt relaxed and positive minded, he proceeded to envision looking at the catcher who was signaling for a slider. Before visualizing going into his windup, Ben took about 20 seconds to find the right grip on the baseball. Once the ball felt right, he imagined slowly going into his windup while in full control of his mechanics; imagined feeling the release of the seams of the ball alongside his fingertips; and imagined hitting his exact target while hearing a 'POP' as the ball smacked into the heart of the catcher's mitt.

At first Ben described feeling "awkward" as he imagined going through the motions during positive imagery. Throwing his slider usually ended badly in the past, so imagining it going well now was unfamiliar to him. This was okay because together we were going to repeat positive imagery enough times to where it would start feeling more comfortable. As we re-practiced positive imagery using the same scenario over and over again, Ben gradually bought into the idea that throwing his slider for a strike consistently was within the realm of possibility. After eight rounds, Ben had rehearsed how to stay calm, keep his thoughts in control, and focus on a positive outcome. Now he was ready to practice using positive imagery on the mound during non-game situations to see if it would help. If it did, this had the potential to boost his confidence during real-game situations.

I requested Ben to practice positive imagery before every single pitch thrown during the offseason. Every. Single. Pitch. I even asked him to practice positive imagery at least once a day at home before going to bed at night. Ben wanted to get back on track so bad that he didn't hesitate to do what I asked. With a new set of tools and a rekindled spirit, he began noticing incremental improvements in pitch accuracy as the offseason progressed. His confidence was building the more he threw his sliders and changeups for strikes. After several months of practicing positive imagery, come Spring training Ben started off hot by striking out 6 of 13 batters. He only walked one.

2: Sensory-Integrated-Imagery-Training

What is Sensory-Integrated-Imagery-Training

If the phrase 'sensory-integrated-imagery-training' sounds intimidating, don't worry. It's just a fancy term I use for a concept that is easy to understand and to apply. Sensory-integrated-imagery-training is very similar to positive imagery. They both simulate difficult situations and end in positive outcomes. However, the two key differences are that sensory-integrated-imagery-training involves going through the actual real-life motions and mechanics (in addition to visualizing a positive outcome), and it incorporates additional stimuli on top of tactile sensations (sound, smell, taste). Thus, we get the term "sensory integration," because we are integrating additional senses into the training experience.

The purpose of adding sound, smell, and/or taste is to make the sensory-integrated-imagery-training experience more realistic. We don't have to hit on all five senses to make sensory-integrated-imagery-training effective. Although, the more senses we stimulate the more profound the brain will recognize these stimuli as *'familiar'* during games. In life, a lack of familiarity can throw us for a loop. Take witnessing a car accident as an example, something we don't see every day. This terrifying experience often induces the sympathetic nervous system to kick in, leading to the fight, flight, or freeze stress response we talked about in chapter three. If we fight (help out in the situation), we are exerting a degree of control over stress. If we flee (avoid the situation), we are running away from stress. If we freeze (are incapacitated), stress paralyzes us. To adequately prepare new EMT's to handle car accidents, they incorporate real-life equipment, gear, and ambulances into their training to recreate realistic simulations. Using sensory-integrated-imagery-training we are doing something similar with athletes. By pre-exposing them to unfamiliar circumstances while coming into contact with relevant stimuli, they will learn to activate their fight response when stress strikes.

An example of how sensory-integrated-imagery-training works involves blasting audio recordings of booing crowds as athletes rehearse to maintain all-around poise. This way, when they face similar situations in real life they are more likely to say to themselves "Hey, I've heard this before, and I know exactly how to handle it." In this regard, sensory-integrated-imagery-training acts as a form of desensitization training. It can help numb athletes of any discomforts when distractions such as loud noises come into play.

Why Sensory-Integrated-Imagery-Training

I am often asked what is the best way to prepare athletes for the toughest situations they have yet to experience. How do you in fact prepare an athlete to control stress in the ninth inning of game 7 of the World Series, maintain focus while putting on the 18th hole at the Masters, or maintain physical composure before a game-winning field goal try in the Super Bowl? Although our opinions may vary, I believe the answer lies mostly in sensory-integrated-imagery-training. If we can't physically experience something on demand, the next best thing we can do is mentally experience it on demand. We do this by using a systematic process of mental rehearsal. This is the core of sensory-integrated-imagery-training. It programs athletes so they now exactly which steps to take when they encounter foreign situations. Unless our athletes are among the few who have already experienced really rare situations, we don't have many other options. Virtual reality would be a terrific alternative. Unfortunately, virtual reality programs are harder to access for many athletes and can be expensive if they have to pay out of pocket. Another option would be for coaches to split a team up into two and simulate an intra-squad game with the intensity as if it were a championship game. Theoretically, this could be very useful. However, it can be hard for coaches to distinguish between which players are buying into this mentality. With sensory-integrated-imagery-training, we are ensuring athletes are adequately prepared for the most intense situations imaginable on the field.

Where Athletes Can Practice Sensory-Integrated-Imagery-Training

Sensory-integrated-imagery-training can be applied in two different ways. The first option is for athletes to rehearse the technique at home. I've always felt practicing imagery techniques is very effective before going to bed, because it consolidates practice into memory. The second option is for athletes to use the strategy on an actual field during non-game situations (practices and scrimmages). Examples of the latter could include a relief pitcher simulating closing out the game in the bottom of the ninth inning during bullpen sessions. A quarterback imagining that a drive during intra-squads is the final drive of the game. A tennis player pretending they are serving in a tie-breaker during a friendly match. Or a golfer pretending each putt is an opportunity to win a tournament. Regardless of the scenarios athletes choose, practices and scrimmages are worthwhile opportunities to incorporate all their new tools into a semi-live setting. Moreover, when athletes utilize sensory-integrated-imagery-rehearsal within multiple settings (on different fields, arenas, or stadiums), it will be easier for them to stick to their guns when they're competing on the road.

As we continue to discuss sensory-integrated-imagery-training in this chapter, we will focus on applying the strategy using the mental rehearsal approach (meaning how they would rehearse the technique at home). Until athletes feel comfortable visually overcoming specific scenarios while going through the actual motions, only then should they consider practicing the technique on an actual field. The last thing we want is for an athlete to jump into something too soon and unprepared, only to come back to tell us it didn't work during practice. This has happened to me only once. I explained that just because someone completes their CPR training doesn't mean they're actually ready to perform real CPR.

Scenarios for Sensory-Integrated-Imagery-Training

As we explore which situations to use, we want to pick one or two different scenarios athletes can envision during sensory-integrated-imagery-training. More than two can be overkill. Choosing two scenarios is beneficial for two reasons. First, it gives athletes more time to focus in-depth on each situation separately, so they can master control and gain sufficient confidence over that situation. Second, when athletes learn how to effectively overcome one situation, they can use the same techniques to overcome other situations. This is called generalizing a skill. When athletes learn to rise above stress in situation A, they can use the same tools to rise above stress in situation B. In other words, if athletes can overcome one situation, they are significantly more likely to overcome other situations that are remotely similar.

Scenarios to consider include any of the trigger situations we identified in Chapter Five (when we discussed *'Identifying Triggers'*). These triggers included current and previous situations when athletes are/were vulnerable to critical mental skills breakdown, or had difficulty managing physical and mental stress symptoms. Other scenario options to consider could include hypothetical moments when we anticipate athletes may struggle. These hypothetical scenarios would test an athlete's mental resiliency and could potentially expose critical mental skills needing continued improvement. For example, if an athlete continues to have confidence issues, we may ask them to imagine a scenario where everyone (including coaches and teammates) are mad at them for making an error. We can think of these hypothetical scenarios in much the same way how a flu shot or an immunization works: by exposing athletes to a low dose in a controlled environment, they are building a "mental immunity" later on down the road.

A great example when we may anticipate future struggles involves rookie athletes. We always hear coaches and analysts talk about experience. "Oh, that veteran has experience." "Oh, that guy knows how to get it done." When it comes to rookie athletes, they simply don't have that same level of experience as their veteran counterparts. Other than the rules of their sport, everything becomes new to them. New surroundings. New teammates. New coaches. New jerseys. Tougher competition. As I mentioned earlier, what is unfamiliar to us can make us uncomfortable. However, those rookies who have thoroughly mentally prepared themselves for their big cameo have a tremendous mental advantage compared to their peers (who probably focused more on their physical preparation instead). Mental preparedness is also a form of "experience," and sensory-integrated-imagery-training is a great way for rookies to bridge this experience gap.

Preparing for Sensory-Integrated-Imagery-Training
As we prepare athletes for sensory-integrated-imagery-training, they will be using all of the performance enhancement strategies they have learned thus far. Some of these strategies will be used en-vivo (used in real-time in front of us). Others will be imagined. For example, athletes will use actual relaxation techniques while maintain strong physical poise characteristics; yet they may internally practice positive self-talk and self-motivational skills in their heads (although around us they should talk us through their thinking patterns so we can monitor them and give feedback). This combination of real life and mental application of skills will be similar to how they will apply the strategy at home and on the field.

Each round of sensory-integrated-imagery-training typically lasts between six to eight minutes. After each attempt, we can take time to review how the experience was for them, what they did well, and how they may improve the next time. As athletes repeat the exercise, they will gradually learn to apply the tools quicker and more efficiently. Most athletes will practice four or five rounds before moving on. It never hurts to practice more than five rounds. I rarely practice less than four rounds because if athletes start getting bored, I want to see how they respond when they are not as motivated!

As athletes imagine their scenarios, it helps to include as much detail as possible into the visualization process. This will recreate a realistic situation they may encounter one day. Whether we describe the characteristics of an arena, sights, smells, sounds, or any other tactile experiences, the visualization process should depict an emotional snapshot in time. The more vividly they can picture what that moment would actually look and feel like, the more familiar it will feel when that time arises.

As we mentioned earlier, sensory-integrated-imagery-training uses sensory objects (stimuli) to make the experience more realistic. When athletes integrate objects during the visualization process, it triggers their brain into remembering what they need to do to thrive. Similarly to when we hear a certain song, or smell a familiar scent, stimuli can evoke our recall memory. It is akin to how a certain song may remind us of a moment in high school, or a particular scent reminds us of a moment in our childhood. For some athletes, sensory stimuli may offer additional comfort because they were associated with a positive experience around us. As coaches, you may need to plan in advance which stimuli you will incorporate into the exercise, especially if you are going to practice sensory-integrated-imagery-training indoors. If you have the means, practicing sensory-integrated-imagery-training on an actual field (or gym, arena, pool, etc) is also a great option, so long as you are there to guide the athlete until they become proficient to practice the strategy on their own.

Sensory objects to consider should include items athletes are exposed to and come into contact with during games. Examples of sensory objects could include: balls; sports equipment; grass; sounds of the game; dirt; bubblegum; Gatorade; and jerseys. Sport-specific objects could include: a baseball; the smell of chlorinated water; a golf club; a tennis racquet; a football helmet; shin guards; a hockey stick; etc.

When to add sensory objects into the process depends on the nature of an athlete's sport. Some athletes may use these objects from the start of the exercise. Others may introduce certain objects at a strategic point during the exercise. For example, a pitcher may grip a baseball the entire time, whereas a quarterback may imagine squatting behind the snapper before feeling the ball in his hands.

How to Apply Sensory-Integrated-Imagery-Training

Once we have identified which scenario to use, which sensory stimuli to incorporate, and when to incorporate these stimuli, we are ready to stand up and begin the exercise. Athletes may keep their eyes open or closed during the process, depending on their preference. I like to have athletes practice both. As we describe the situation, they will begin going through the motions to simulate their mechanics. This means going into their windup, lobbing a tennis ball in the air on a serve, or getting into their stance on a golf drive.

As athletes walk us through the stages, it becomes a collaborative process as we monitor their problem solving skills, thinking patterns, and offer feedback. Even as athletes incrementally modify their approach, there is usually room for continual improvement. Athletes will have plenty of chances to perfect their approach through repeated role-plays.

As we start initial role-plays, we may request athletes to describe the sensory stimuli they are using. This is to cue them in case they need to make any physical adjustments when coming into contact with an object. If something in the body or mind feels off, they can adjust and get more comfortable. For example, if a baseball player is gripping the bat too tightly, they can pause and loosen up their grip. If a basketball player gets distracted by the prerecorded boos of a crowd, they can take a moment to redirect their focus onto the texture of the ball. Or if a soccer player has negative mini mental flashbacks, they can concentrate on the patterns of the ball to facilitate grounding.

At the end of each role-play, athletes should end the experience by visualizing a positive outcome to promote positive feelings and positive thoughts. Like positive imagery, athletes have the flexibility in choosing their specific positive outcome as long as it's achievable on the field.

After each round of sensory-integrated-imagery-training, we can continue providing feedback on ways to improve. Until athletes demonstrate they can apply all the skills on their own without hesitation, they will be ready to practice the technique outside of session. If athletes continue to need our feedback, we may re-practice the strategy as many times as needed until they get it down.

To simplify the steps of sensory-integrated-imagery-training, the following is a step-by-step outline you may follow:

1) Identify which scenario to use (pick one or two situations)
2) Review which performance enhancement strategies athletes will apply to manage the situation
3) Select specific sensory objects to incorporate (you may include multiple items); more is better
4) Set up the scenario by describing the events leading up to the moment
5) Ask athletes to stand up, go through the motions, and talk us through which strategies they are using
6) Ask them about the stimuli they are using, including how they may adapt and feel more comfortable while exposed to it
7) Provide feedback during each attempt
8) Have the athlete end by visualizing a positive outcome
9) After each attempt, ask the athlete how the experience was for them, what they did well, and how they may improve the next time
10) Repeat practice of sensory-integrated-imagery-training scenarios until athletes can apply performance enhancement techniques without our help

Case Example
The following is a case study how I applied sensory-integrated-imagery-training in the past, using "Brett" as our example:

Brett was a freshman shortstop for an elite Division I collegiate program. Highly recruited out of high school by the top colleges throughout the nation, Brett decided to attend a top-fifteen nationally ranked baseball program. Unfortunately, Brett was second string behind an All-American Junior, who was having another spectacular year. Brett was eager to get his "feet wet" and get his first at-bat, but he had no idea when this opportunity would come.

Brett approached me to help him prepare for his first at-bat, which he felt was looming. He wanted to give himself the best opportunity for success once that chance arrived.

Brett's sensory-integrated-imagery-training session involved using a baseball bat, helmet, gum, and grass. At this stage in time we had already worked five weeks together and he was fully prepared for sensory-integrated-imagery-training. The scenario we chose was a casual moment in the game when Brett was in the dugout with his teammates. In this instance, Brett was anticipating getting his first at-bat. Since this was the first time he had practiced sensory-integrated-imagery-training, I spent more time than usual walking him through each step of the experience to help guide him the first time around.

> Coach: "Imagine you are inside your home dugout. You see all the familiar advertisements and banners around the field selling their products. You can hear the fans in the crowd chatting in the background, but you can't make out what any of them are saying. You smell the freshly cut grass and notice how green it is [I proceed to hand Brett a handful of grass to smell]. You look up in the stands and see a dad with his son sharing a bag of peanuts. You see the hotdog man selling his hotdogs. And your cap fits snuggly on your head. It's late in the game, and your team is up by six runs. You look around, soaking it all in. The umpires are all dressed in black as usual. Your jersey is white and clean, because you haven't had the opportunity to get in the game yet. You're standing by the edge of the dugout, cheering your teammates on. And then… suddenly…coach turns to you…and in his raspy voice mumbles, "Brett, grab a bat." What are you thinking and feeling at this moment?"
>
> Brett: "I'm feeling really excited because I'm finally getting my chance. But I'm also feeling a bit nervous because I don't want to screw it up. I want to go out there and show coach what I can do."
>
> Coach: "You're feeling nervous? You don't want to screw it up? What are you going to do to feel less nervous?"

Brett: *"I'm going to breathe deeply, maybe stretch my arms and legs a little. You know...to start getting loose."* [Brett proceeds to stretch out his arms and legs]

Coach: *"And you said you don't want to screw up your chance. Is that statement going to help?"*

Brett: *"No. I guess not. I have to think more positive. This is my chance to show coach."*

Coach: *"Good. So now, right after your coach turned to you to grab your bat, you look around at your teammates, and are feeling pretty excited." What do you think would happen next?"*

Brett: *"I'm sure my teammates would say something. Maybe like 'atta baby' or 'go get em.' I'm sure they'd be excited for me."*

Coach: *"I would be excited for you, too. So what do you think would happen after that?"*

Brett: *"I'd walk over, grab my bat, put on my helmet, and start walking out of the dugout.* [At this point Brett grabs a bat and helmet beside him; he puts the helmet on his head, and begins gripping the bat with both hands, squeezing the grip].

Coach: *"Hold the bat like you would normally* [Brett adjusts his grip of the bat]. *How does the helmet feel on your head?"*

Brett: *"It feels good."*

Coach: *"How does that bat feel in your hands?"*

Brett: *"It feels right."* [Brett loosens his grip on the bat while strumming his fingers]

Coach: *"Now that the helmet feels nicely snug on your head, and you're gripping the bat normally, imagine that you take your first steps out of the dugout. And just as you reach the top of the dugout, and hit the dirt, what always happens?*

Brett: *"Um, I don't know. What?"*

Coach: *"What do you hear?"*

Brett: *"Um...my coach? My teammates? I don't know."*

Coach: *"No, that's not what I'm looking for. What do you hear when your cleats hit the dirt?"*

Brett: "Oh, I hear a crunch."
Coach: "Yes, you hear a crunch! So now you're out of the dugout, and take slow, confident strides towards the on-deck circle. And every step you take, you hear a crunch, after crunch. Finally you reach the on-deck circle. What do you usually do next?"
Brett: "I pick up the donut (bat weight), and put it on my bat."
Coach: "Then what do you do?"
Brett: "I start taking a few hacks (swings) to loosen up." [Brett takes two, slow simulated swings of the bat]
Coach: "So you're taking your hacks. What kinds of thoughts are going through your head?"
Brett: "I'm trying to stay focused on the pitcher. Trying to prepare myself for my at-bat."
Coach: "What other feelings are you experiencing?"
Brett: "I'm feeling my heart begin to race a little. Honestly, I would still feel a little bit nervous."
Coach: "So what can you do to feel less nervous?"
Brett: "Well I'm focusing on my breathing. I guess I can try and focus more on the situation instead of my body."
Coach: "What can you do to focus away from your body? Do you remember any of the other techniques we talked about?"
Brett: "Um...oh yeah. I can focus on the spot on my bat." [This is a Band-Aid focusing strategy discussed in chapter eight under focus: by placing a small dot on his bat with a sharpie, Brett would spin his bat while in the on-deck circle, stare up at the bat, and then focus all of his attention onto finding that small dot].
Brett: [Brett takes several actual deep breaths, stretches his neck side to side, and squeezes the handle of the bat. Brett proceeds to spin the bat in his hands en-vivo and locates the dot].
Coach: "Excellent. So now you're using that *dot to focus and tune everything else out. You're completely fixated on that dot. Is there anything else you can do to continue to prepare even more?*
Brett: "Um, I'm not sure."

Coach: *"How about some positive imagery. How would that help?"*
Brett: *"Oh yeah. That would help me rehearse seeing the ball and taking solid hacks at it."*
Coach: *"So now you're imagining seeing the ball and taking quality swings. Each time you swing, you remember how sweet it feels when the ball perfectly hits the barrel of the bat. What a beautiful sound it makes: that 'ping.' After remembering how those 'pings' feel and sound, you look up towards the pitcher to watch his stuff. On the next pitch, you notice your teammate hits a grounder up the middle for a hit. Guess what? You're up! How are you going to approach the plate?"*
Brett: *"I'm going to walk up confidently, take my breaths, and keep imagining seeing each pitch. I'm going to stay focused and within myself."*
Coach: *"OK, so now you're at the plate, the pitcher is staring down at the catcher. Maybe you make eye contact with each other for a brief moment. You take one step into the batter's box, and then another. You settle into your stance. You're feeling relaxed and focused. You watch the pitcher set, go into his windup, and here it comes. What's going through your mind?"*
Brett: *"I'm focused on the ball coming out of the pitcher's hand. I'm saying to myself: 'see the ball, see the ball.'"*
Coach: *"Just then, you watch the ball sizzling by you for a strike. What's going through your mind to prepare for the next pitch?"*
Brett: *"I'm thinking I could hit this guy and I want him to throw it again."*
Coach: *"You get back into the box for the next pitch. You're still focused, and carefully watch the pitcher setting himself again. He goes into the windup, and delivers. You see the ball like it's a giant melon, and you take a comfortable rip. Next thing you know you feel that solid 'ping' as you drive it squarely up the middle for a single. As you get to first base, you hear your teammates cheering for you. Congratulations. How does it feel?"*
Brett: *"It feels great. I think I can make that happen in real life."*

The second time around I talked a lot less as Brett talked me through each step of the process. Like most athletes, he needed my initial help to add visual details. Additionally, he needed a few reminders on which performance enhancement techniques to use. After four attempts, Brett showed me he could guide himself through the visualization process without my help. This indicated that he was prepared to practice sensory-integrated-imagery-training on his own, both on the field during practice, and at home.

A month after committing to practicing sensory-integrated-imagery-training on his own five times per week, Brett eventually got his first at-bat. Although Brett struck out, he walked in his second at-bat, and singled in his third. The day after getting his first hit, Brett called to report that as soon as he felt that "*crunch*" of his cleats digging into the dirt, he was instantly reminded of our work together and experienced a heightened sense of confidence. More importantly, Brett now had a powerful tool he could rely on for the rest of his career.

End of Session Six

At the end of session six we can assign athletes homework to simulate positive imagery during practices and scrimmages daily, and to practice sensory-integrated-imagery-training at least three times per week.

CHAPTER 7

Session 7: Skills Review and Prevention Planning

> *"An ounce of prevention is worth a pound of cure."*
> -BENJAMIN FRANKLIN

Overview of Session Seven

Session seven may be our last meeting with athletes face-to-face. If you used this SPET model from beginning to end, you should have observed an evolution in an athlete's mental game over the past six weeks. We started by planting important mental seeds. We watched their mental approach bloom. Now we want their mental skills to flourish.

Newly strengthened mental skills endure so long as athletes remain committed to applying recently incorporated mental performance enhancement strategies on a consistent basis. One of the pitfalls is when athletes notice significant improvements and then prematurely stop using our strategies based on the belief that all their problems are solved. In these situations, the chances of relapse are much higher. Athletes who return to old habits that didn't work in the first place run the risk of renewed struggles. One of the goals of prevention planning is to reduce this risk of relapse. As for non-SPET coaches, prevention planning can be a method to occasionally check-in with athletes to ensure they are continuing to incorporate important tools into their routines. This can be done in the locker room, on the sideline, in the dugout, on a team flight, etc.

Prevention planning also tests whether athletes are prepared to overcome upcoming performance challenges independently. Unexpected challenges will likely arise. When they do, we want to ensure they know how to problem solve on their own. The quicker they apply SPET strategies on the field, the easier it will be for them to remain mentally sound. Regardless of your role working with athletes, this entire chapter is applicable to you because we won't be starting with our usual check-in.

At the Start of Session Seven

1) Review homework: to practice positive imagery on the field daily; and to practice sensory-integrated-imagery-training three times during the week

As we begin session seven, we won't be checking-in regarding progress towards goals, or review green flags and red flags at the onset. These topics will be covered separately as part of our agenda for the day. I like to start by checking-in on their homework from last session: to practice positive imagery on the field during practices and scrimmages daily; and to practice sensory-integrated-imagery-training at least three times during the week. Having practiced these dynamic visualization techniques is crucial because they will engrain mental performance techniques into their routines. Many athletes will have completed the assignment. In my experience, athletes who practiced these techniques more often tend to outperform those who don't. If athletes failed to follow-through on their assignment, this may be the last chance for SPET coaches to get them to start using visualization techniques.

Content of Session Seven

1: Re-Assess Newly Strengthened Critical Mental Skills
2: Goal Outcomes
3: Reviewing Green Flags and Red Flags
4: Skills Review
5: Prevention Planning

1: Re-Assess Newly Strengthened Critical Mental Skills

Re-evaluating each of the ten critical mental skills will help us determine whether athletes are ready to move on without us. If critical mental skills needing initial improvement are no longer hurting performance, we can move on with our prevention planning agenda. If critical mental skills continue to negatively impact performance, we may want to consider working with athletes a little while longer (perhaps at least another week or two). The last thing we want is to send athletes into the arena alone knowing they continue to have mental loopholes. Re-evaluating critical mental skills lets us gauge their status before moving on.

Many athletes will have strengthened at least half of their critical mental skills. This is what we as coaches should strive towards. When athletes improve five or more critical mental skills, their progress is typically reflected in their performance statistics (that is unless we worked with athletes during the off-season or during an injury). Basketball players should have upped their shooting percentage. Quarterbacks should have increased their completion percentage. And pitchers should have lowered their earned-run-averages. Although solidifying all ten critical mental skills is ideal, the impact of improving five or more critical mental skills should be evident in one form or another. Going over these impacts is a great way to inspire athletes to keep the momentum going and to stick to SPET strategies.

Very few athletes will have improved four or less critical mental skills. The general exception would be when athletes already had strong mental skills to begin with, yet simply wanted to take their mental game to the next level. As we monitored their continual progress each session, kept track of goals and flags, checked-in with weekly homework assignments, and incorporated Band-Aid strategies, athletes should have improved all critical mental skills requiring improvement. If they did not, it's typically because they either did not put in 100% effort, or because there were deeper underlying issues at play, such as personal circumstances out of our control. In these cases, we may want to pinpoint what went wrong in case there is any way to salvage their situation. Fortunately, in my experience these cases are very rare.

2: Goal Outcomes

In session two, we helped athletes identify one to two goals to strive towards. Each session thereafter, we monitored goal progress to measure the efficacy of SPET strategies. While there should be no surprises as we assess for goal outcomes at this time, highlighting their final goal status can be an additional tool to inspire a continued dedication and commitment to relying on SPET strategies.

When athletes reach their goals, we want to praise them and make a big deal out of it. This celebrates their achievement and reaffirms how hard work pays off. It shows athletes that when they keep their eye on the prize, they are capable of accomplishing what they set out to seek. Equally important is to give athletes all the credit for their success. This sends the message that they don't need us around to be successful anymore. As coaches, we gave athletes a diving board from which to leap off. We supplied them with an array of tools and they put these tools into action. It was the athlete who welcomed the diving board and jumped off it.

In cases when athletes report partial progress, this is also an accomplishment. We may anticipate some athletes to improve a bulk of their critical mental skills, yet still fall short of reaching their goals. Sometimes hitting goals just needs a little more time since they only had seven weeks to incrementally apply SPET tools and strategies. Even partial success demonstrates that the athlete was committed to making changes in their game. With an ongoing dedication to using SPET strategies, reaching goals is a very realistic outcome.

3: Reviewing Green Flags and Red Flags

Session seven is our last opportunity to review green flags and red flags. These flags were used to identify pre-game factors that were either positively or negatively spilling over onto the field at the start of games. In many cases, athletes will have identified several flags. They will have applied specific strategies to increase the frequency of green flags while reducing the frequency of red flags. For a few athletes, flags were never an issue. Either way, we want to rehash the importance of flag identification and manipulation one last time so athletes can add it into their mental tool box of strategies.

4: Skills Review

The purpose of skills review is to revisit each of the strategies athletes can use on the field so they become permanently engrained into their heads. Going over the various strategies is a great time to remind athletes why each strategy works, when to use them, and how other strategies can be simultaneously combined to maximize their potency. Athletes will likely remember most of the strategies we review. If they don't, skills review will remind them of the strategies they may have forgotten. Strategies to review would include:

1) Flag Identification and Goal Setting
2) Relaxation and Stress Management Skills: Mindfulness, Deep Breathing, Muscle relaxation, and Grounding
3) Positive Thinking: Thought Stopping and Positive Self-Talk
4) All-Round Poise: Awareness of Composure and the Mind-Body Connection
5) Positive Imagery and Sensory-Integrated-Imagery-Training
6) Any Band-Aid strategies

5: Prevention Planning

Prevention planning tests an athlete's preparedness to overcome mental performance challenges independently. It uses hypothetical scenarios to measure how quickly they can identify which performance enhancement strategies to use at any given time. Furthermore, it's an additional way to etch each strategy deeper into their brains to galvanize their recall memory.

Prevention planning involves quizzing athletes to test how they would handle difficult situations in the future. In a way, these quizzes are similar to a final exam before graduating. In our case, we can assist them during the process if they need help. The more scenarios we throw at them, the quicker they should respond as to how they would problem solve each dilemma. By the time we're done we want these strategies to become instinctive so athletes can focus on executing plays on the field rather than pausing to ponder which strategies to use. Once athletes fire off which strategies they would apply, without our help, they have passed the test.

Hypothetical scenarios include any situation that could potentially impair all-around poise in the future. This includes situations when any of the 10 critical mental skills or physical composure becomes vulnerable. You can create your own hypothetical scenarios if needed, as long as they are relevant to your athlete and their sport. Or you may offer specific situations in the past when athletes have struggled to test if they remember how to tackle these situations differently the next time. I recommend both of these options. Here are some hypothetical scenarios you may ask your athlete:

"You just made a costly mistake. How are you going to rebound from the situation on the next play?"

"You're in a tight spot in the game, and you notice your heart racing really fast. What can you do?"

"You notice your legs starting to tense up. What would help?"

"You feel nervous in 'X' situation. How are you going to remain relaxed and focused?"

"You've had a horrible first half and feel frustrated. How will you maintain your composure at the start of the second half?"

"You're starting to doubt yourself because your opponent is on fire. How will you remain competitive and continue giving it your all?"

"You're upset because the referee/umpire just made a terrible call. How will you maintain your focus?"

"You're in a two-week long slump. What would help you snap out of it?"

When athletes answer to each hypothetical scenario with fast responses, they've successfully incorporated the strategies into their reactive thinking. These athletes are ready for life without us. However, when athletes take longer to think, we may want to continue quizzing them until naming specific strategies becomes easier.

End of Session Seven
Once we are done quizzing athletes and are satisfied with the results, we have completed what we initially set off to accomplish: to teach them all the tools they need to achieve long-lasting mental soundness. At this time, we want athletes to feel confident that they don't need us anymore. Some athletes will be eager to move on. Others may be more hesitant or uncomfortable with the idea. If athletes feel the latter, we want to highlight their progress to encourage them to try using their new skills independently. If athletes can sustain success on the field after leaving our office for the last time, their confidence will grow faster as they build self-efficacy. As athletes walk off into the sunset, they should feel a peace of mind knowing that they now possess the mental tools they need to be successful.

CHAPTER 8

Band-Aid Strategies

What are Band-Aids

Band-Aids that we stick on our bodies are designed to protect open wounds by reducing the risk of exposure to germs and bacteria. *"Mental Band-Aids"* are similar to real Band-Aids because they are meant to prevent athletes from experiencing further harm by facilitating healing. Mental Band-Aids are temporary quick-fix solutions used to stop the bleeding. Although they can be very effective when used on their own, they are supplemental strategies athletes can use that become even more powerful when combined with other SPET techniques.

Each Band-Aid strategy targets specific critical mental skills. Depending on which critical mental skills need improvement, you may consider using Band-Aids at anytime. When athletes are experiencing urgent mental performance issues, Band-Aids will add to the athlete's mental tool box of strategies. Similarly to how a repairman relies on his tool box of hammers, screwdrivers, and nails to fix objects, mental Band-Aids can be used to fine-tune mental skills.

Three of the critical mental skills are intentionally left out of the Band-Aids chapter. These include positive self-talk, stress management and coping skills, and personal goal setting. These skills were already talked about at length in previous chapters [see chapter 2, chapter 3, chapter 4]. However, if you feel more can be done to address these omitted critical skills, you can always design your own Band-Aids as needed. In many cases, coming up with your own Band-Aids just takes a bit of creativity and ingenuity.

Confidence

People have a strong tendency to overestimate their strengths and underestimate their weaknesses. This is especially true when it comes to reporting confidence levels, which is often a defense mechanism to avoid feelings of dejection and demoralization. If we determine an athlete's confidence levels are in serious need for improvement, we have to be cautious with our approach. Instead of blatantly calling them out on it, a more prudent approach would be to subtly point out that confidence needs improvement; followed by supplying them with confidence Band-Aids to add to their repertoire. The following are some confidence-building Band-Aid strategies to consider.

A Reality-Check

For some athletes, a string of recent on-field struggles can cause them to engage in thoughts of self-doubt. When you're not performing up to par, self-doubt can creep in and lead to a downward spiral in confidence. Athletes who begin losing their confidence risk becoming engrossed in negative memories revolving around these recent failures, similar to those mini mental flashbacks we talked about earlier. This can be a very embarrassing and lonely experience. Fortunately, we can use *reality checks* to help athletes think more critically and reexamine their situation in order to re-instill feelings of hope.

When athletes start losing confidence it helps to start off by hearing the athlete out; to understand why they are feeling doubtful; and to hear what triggered their lack of confidence. Through listening and understanding athletes will feel emotionally supported by us and perhaps even feel some degree of relief. Once we have a better understanding, we can begin challenging their beliefs by diluting their negative memories with more positive ones. Instead of focusing on their recent failures, we will refocus their attention onto what's been going right. This includes even small successes on the field. Research shows that when people remember their track record of success, they are more likely to feel confident under similar circumstances. With athletes, the more they remember their achievements today, the more likely they will feel better about their situation tomorrow.

I worked with a college wide-receiver who always felt overmatched when paired against a certain opposing cornerback. This wide-receiver had the preexisting notion that since he was unsuccessful the last two times, he was destined to get shutdown by him again. On top of that, this cornerback was quicker, faster, and stronger than he was. As we explored moments in previous games when he was successful against this cornerback, he mentioned one catch where he broke open for a 37-yard reception. At that moment he had a cathartic experience and realized success against this opponent was possible and could come at anytime. He followed up this realization by saying "You know, I've beaten that guy a few times before, I think I can do it again." Sure enough, he scored a touchdown against that same opponent the next time they faced each other.

Highlight Continual Progress

Highlighting progress, including even small increments of progress, can foster confidence. When we notice any gains, we are more likely to feel hopeful and positive about our situation. This becomes a self-perpetuating process: as we feel more positively and hopeful, our self-confidence improves knowing that we're headed in the right direction. In a way, paying attention to our progress can provide us with our own built-in moral support. It can help us stay steady towards the pursuit of our dreams and ambitions.

There are several ways to determine progress, each of which can be used to promote confidence. These methods include: progress towards goals; improved performance statistics; strengthened mental skills; increased strength and agility; increased usage of mental performance strategies; more playing time; a promotion; a bump in salary; etc. As we explore each of these categories, the more progress we can point out, the better athletes will feel about their situation.

Showing Attitude
By showing "attitude" on the field, I don't mean acting overly cocky. Showing attitude means showing strong body language and poise that from an outside perspective looks as though you are determined to win. Showing attitude can additionally become a longer lasting mindset using the "fake it till you make it" approach. In some cases, if you trick your body into thinking you are confident, it can give you that extra boost of needed energy. If athletes use the technique and begin experiencing immediate success on the field, it can transform into real authentic confidence if sustained long enough.

The other benefit of showing attitude is that exuding confidence simply feels good, even if it's not completely authentic. When we pretend to feel good, our mind has a better chance to follow course. It can send a message to opponents that, "Hey, this guy looks hungry and determined." Coaches love that.

The Golden Gift Theory
The golden gift theory is a temporary Band-Aid strategy that may be useful when athletes are experiencing current struggles on the field. For this Band-Aid athletes pretend they hold a "magical object" related to their sport whose "enchanted qualities" guarantee to improve their success. The intention behind the strategy is to spark temporary confidence where athletes can rely on a "golden object" to pull them through. In baseball, a "golden bat" can help a hitter get out of a slump because it "promises" hits. In football it can be "golden receiver" gloves that will improve catching abilities. In basketball it can be a "golden hand" that improves accuracy during free throws. In soccer it can be a "golden foot." If this golden gift idea sounds absurd, you're not alone. However, it may be worth a shot if an athlete is

in a rut. A brief word of caution though, this Band-Aid should be used on fewer occasions, such as when athletes feel like they are running out of other options.

Desire for Personal On-Field Success

A desire for personal on-field success may be a bit more challenging to improve for some athletes. Some athletes are more humble compared to others, or aren't as interested in reaping all the rewards of personal glory. Additionally, the nature of the competition also plays a role; some sports are more group-oriented, whereas other sports are individualized (i.e. tennis and golf). Therefore, how athletes define personal success will vary from one athlete to another. For those athletes who may benefit from improving their desire for personal success, we may consider the following Band-Aids to enhance or rekindle their desire.

Remembering How Success Felt

One approach to restoring a desire for personal on-field success is by helping athletes remember how good success felt in the past. By reliving past positive experiences, we hope to inspire athletes into wanting to relive these moments again in the future. Remembering the positive feelings, positive emotions, rush of adrenalin, or the sense of personal accomplishment associated with success can be used to inspire athletes to reach for those experiences again. Knowing which aspects of success athletes enjoy the most can be our bait to lure them back towards a desire for personal success. Areas of success athletes typically enjoy include: a celebratory Gatorade bath; a performance bonus; the satisfaction of winning; positive memories; the roar of the crowd; or a championship ring; single handedly clinching the game, etc. Finding out which perks related to success they find rewarding can motivate athletes to strive for these same rewards again in the future.

"Reverse Psychology"

When we hear the term "reverse psychology," most of us automatically know what this means. When we use reverse psychology we are provoking people into doing the exact opposite of what we are telling them to do. In other words, we are instigating them to choose one stance instead of another, hoping they will make the right choice in the end. As we play the role of the devil's advocate we are taking the position that athletes are not interested in personal success. When they feel attacked, they tend to defend themselves by arguing the flip side. Ultimately, it is not us who needs the convincing. Rather, reverse psychology is an opportunity for athletes to critically examine why their desire for personal success in important.

As we consider using reverse psychology, keep in mind that we should always let athletes know when we are using the technique. The last thing we want is for athletes to feel ambushed and think to themselves, "Who are you? I thought you were on my side." Before using reverse psychology we should let them know what is coming so we can maintain their trust and a good relationship.

The following is an example of how I used reverse psychology in the past. I used reverse psychology to challenge an athlete's "blah" attitude regarding his athletic ambition. This athlete reported that the privilege of competing in his sport was satisfying enough, and that his desire for personal success was less important. The actual conversation lasted six minutes, but I've condensed it to keep it brief:

> Athlete: *"I accept when the other team wins. It's not that I don't want it. If we win, we win. If we lose, we lose."*
> Coach: *"Yeah, I think the other team is ok with that, too. Don't you?"*
> Athlete: *"I'm not too concerned about them. I just do my thing"*
> Coach: *"I'm sure the other team is not worried about you either. I'm sure they love playing against you because they enjoy dominating you. I'm sure after the game they're feeling pretty good, thanks*

to your lack of personal will. You think they talk about you after the game?"

Athlete: "That would be messed up. That would make me upset."

Coach: "That would make me upset, too. But it sounds like you don't really care."

Athlete: "I do care. I'm just not going to lose sleep over it."

Coach: "Yeah, you've got more important things to think about when you're on the field. Like about your dating life, or what you'll be eating for dinner that night."

Athlete: "I just go out there and play."

Coach: "Who would you rather win a head-to-head match up: you, or them? Because I'm pretty sure they want it more."

Athlete: "That's not true. I want it, too."

Coach: "How do you know you want it more? Because you're definitely not convincing anybody."

Athlete: "No, I want it. It just hasn't been my focus."

Coach: "Well, it's the other team's focus. That gives them a competitive advantage over you."

Athlete: "Well maybe. I guess I never thought about it that way. But in the end, the best team usually wins."

Coach: "If you think that, let me ask you a question: If two evenly matched teams are playing against each other, who do you think would be more likely to win: the team that wants it more, or the team that doesn't care as much?"

Athlete: "Probably the team that wants it more."

Coach: "Exactly. And the other team wants it more. Not you."

Athlete: "That's not true. I want it, too."

Coach: "Well. Then prove it."

Athlete: "I want to win. It's not like I'm happy with losing. I like when I play well, it makes me feel good at the end of the day."

Coach: "It still doesn't sound like you're that interested in your own success on the field."

Athlete: "I want to be successful. It makes me feel good."

Coach: *"Aha! So how will you approach the next game differently if you say you want to experience success?"*
Athlete: *"I guess I can go out there more determined and give it my all."*

In the case of this athlete, he felt compelled to defend himself when I told him he wasn't interested in personal success. Although he knew I was using reverse psychology, he felt challenged and wanted to prove me wrong. By gradually playing upon his natural competitive instincts, he eventually discovered that winning was an important part of his personal success. In the following weeks he adjusted his mental mindset by showing more attitude and by putting more intensity into competing.

Dedication and Commitment to the Game

The amount of time and effort an athlete spends on improving their game can reveal their level of dedication and commitment to their sport. Athletes who are continuously willing to enhance training regimens and modify current routines show they are committed and dedicated towards maximizing their potential. When athlete's need improvement in this regards, here are some Band-Aids to consider.

Learning From The Best

Learning from the best lets athletes compare their routines and regimens to those who are the most successful at their level. When athletes study the techniques and tactics used by the best, they can explore which of these strategies will complement their own skillset. These strategies can then be integrated into their own approach to hone skills further. The vast majority of athletes will not have the natural athletic ability of NBA Legend Michael Jordan or Olympic Gold Medalist Natalie Coughlin. Fortunately, talent potential doesn't have to set a limit upon which strategies and techniques athletes can adopt. The time and dedication towards continually improving athletes put in is the surest way for them to maximize their potential. This often helps certain athletes overachieve despite not being as strong or as fast compared to other athletes, and it helps others remain competitive at elite levels.

To illustrate how athletes may incorporate training regimens used by some of the best we can use MLB stars Tony Gwynn and Barry Bonds as examples. Bonds and Gwynn would mark up a baseball with a pen, scribble different letters or numbers on the ball, and then focus on which symbol they last saw before whacking each pitch. This technique sharpens *accommodation* of the eyes, which is the ability to maintain clear focus on a moving object. It doesn't have to read "Bonds" or "Gwynn" on the back of your jersey to benefit from this strategy. Many athletes of different shapes and sizes can try this technique out and see if it works for them (obviously as long as there is some pre-existing degree of hand-eye coordination).

Competitive Edge

A competitive edge can include any attributes athletes bring onto the field to give them an advantage over their opponents. These attributes may include a combination of strength, agility, speed, polished mechanics, training routines, sports IQ, or any critical mental strengths they bring to the table. MLB Pitcher Greg Maddux is a great example of an athlete who had a competitive advantage over other athletes. Despite only throwing 85 miles-per-hour, the accuracy of his pitches, the movement of his pitches, his mechanics, his baseball IQ, and his knowledge of hitters turned him into a Hall of Fame pitcher. It is rumored that he was so baseball-smart that he could predict the exact outcome of an at-bat, pitch-by-pitch.

Listing Strengths

Listing strengths means writing down which special attributes athletes offer, including physical and mental strengths. General physical strengths can include: speed; agility; strength; eye focus; hand-eye coordination; endurance; instincts; and reflexes. Sport-specific physical strengths may include: the ability to rebound basketballs; the ability to bunt baseballs; accuracy on free kicks; tackling skills; serve and volleying in tennis; or putting in golf. Mental strengths would include any of the ten critical mental skills. As athletes write down their strengths and look at them on paper, they may begin to notice they have more to offer than they previously realized. This helps athletes feel better about their situation, which allows them to take advantage of these skills during games.

Ability to Self-Motivate:
Most of us don't enjoy wallowing in self-pity, and most of us don't enjoy rowing the "woe is me" boat. Obsessing over our failures does us little good, but when athletes learn from their mistakes and look at the future as a new opportunity, they will have an easier time staying motivated.

Self Reflection
Self-reflection is a way for athletes to look deep inside themselves to decide what kind of athlete they want to be. Do they want to be the type of athlete who never gives up? Or are they comfortable with being the type that gets knocked down and stays down? Self-reflection allows athletes to critically examine their self-motivational style, including whether their current self-motivation style is helping or hurting performance. Every athlete will tell us they would prefer to be resilient in the face of adversity. However, when athletes have a hard time self-motivating we may point out this contradiction between wants (the desire to remain motivated) and actions (previous inabilities to self-motivate). Further, revealing this contradiction usually increases their awareness that their self-motivational style needs to change.

Mirroring other Athletes
Think back for a moment to when you were a kid. Most of us had sports role models we looked up to and admired. Many of us tried to emulate

these athletes. Some of us adopted similar mechanics. Others may have worn the same jersey numbers. Taking after these role models doesn't have to end once we enter adulthood. Even as adults we can continue modeling after certain athletes by adapting similar characteristics as long as they will benefit us. This is especially true when we observe the self-motivational styles of some of the best athletes. Athletes can mimic the traits and mannerisms of other athletes if they think it will improve their own motivational skills.

When we watch athletes with intense competitive spirits, it's usually safe to assume their ability to self-motivate is equivalent. These athletes have a *reason* to remain competitive. Take former NFL Green Bay Packers quarterback Brett Favre for example. Favre was the master of self-motivational embodiment, having engineered 30 4th-quarter comeback drives. Using Favre as the example, other athletes may consider taking on a similar style and demeanor similar to Favre if they feel it would improve their own ability to self-motivate. Should athletes consider mirroring other athletes, it would be important for them to study the traits and characteristics of those athletes whom they want to emulate after.

Comparing Debbie Downer to Positive Pat

Debbie Downer is always wallowing in self-pity and feeling sorry for herself. Positive Pat always stays positive and keeps her head up. Comparing Debbie Downer to Positive Pat can help athletes clearly see the two extremes of the self-motivational spectrum. Debbie Downer is focused on her failures. Positive Pat is optimistic and hopeful. This spectrum offers athletes two distinct perspectives. One is far more desirable than the other. Athletes always respond that they would rather emulate Positive Pat, and are turned off by Debbie Downer. So the next time an athlete acts like a Debbie Downer, they can say to themselves, "How can I be more like Positive Pat?" The more positive athletes can feel, the more likely they are to maintain higher levels of motivation to compete.

Passion for the Game

Improving a passion for the game can at times be a challenge. Some athletes have valid reasons for their lack of passion, including wanting to spend more time with family, not enjoying all the travel, competing simply because they're good at their sport, or because they have other aspirations and interests they want to pursue. Most athletes have a natural affinity for their sport. But when athletes disclose a lack of passion because something about the game is turning them off, we should explore whether there are fixable solutions.

Internal Triggers, Internal Solutions; External Triggers, External Solutions

Understanding why athletes are losing an interest in their sport can be a tricky process, often because they have more reasons than one. Getting to the root of their underlying reasons will help us offer better solutions to improve their situation. In order to do so, it can be helpful to break down their reasons for their lack of interest into two categories: *internal triggers* or *external triggers*.

Internal Triggers are emotional reasons for their lack of passion and may be the trickier to solve. When we use the word "internal," we mean those feelings, patterns of thinking, and mindsets that take place inside the athlete's mind. Athletes who experience internal triggers justify to themselves that something about their sport isn't fun anymore. When this happens, negative thoughts and negative feelings about their sport begin to outweigh their positive thoughts and feelings towards their sport. Burn-out is an example when negative thoughts and feelings have escalated to the point of little enjoyment. Burn-out typically occurs when athletes overly focus on what they dislike about their sport, which casts their sport in a perpetual negative light. When athletes experience burn-out, their sport becomes more of a burden than a source of pleasure.

External triggers are caused by outside influences, or factors outside of an athlete's control. External triggers can include: pressure from coaches and parents; exhaustion from the constant travel; media criticism; the demanding nature of a sport (such as the rigors of football on the physical body); recurring injuries; and so on. These external triggers can turn athletes off by ruining what used to be fun.

Once we categorize whether triggers are external or internal, we can start customizing a plan to identify potential solutions. Internal solutions are ways to solve internal triggers; while external solutions are ways to solve external triggers.

Internal solutions can be used to help athletes rediscover positive thoughts and feelings towards their sport. We may improve an athlete's outlook by refocusing their attention away from the negative aspects and back onto the positive aspects. Questions we can ask to stimulate positive reflection may include: What things about your sport do you enjoy the most? Give me a recent time when you enjoyed playing? Think back to your earliest memories of the sport – do you remember what led you to fall in love with it in the first place? If you never played the sport again, what would you miss the most about it? Questions such as these can help remind athletes there are still positive aspects of the game they continue to enjoy. These questions also serve to take their focus off their negative thoughts and feelings so they may consider other more positive perspectives.

External solutions are designed to minimize the influence of outside factors that impact one's enjoyment for their sport. At times, coming up with external solutions may require some problem solving. Some external solutions may be solved using mental performance enhancement strategies. For example, if athletes are easily rattled by opposing fans, they can rely on focusing skills, positive self-talk, and sensory-integrated-imagery-training to tune fans out. But when SPET strategies are ineffective at solving external triggers we may have to explore additional solutions. For example, if an athlete is tired of the constant travel, we may recommend they bring certain items on the road to make traveling a bit more enjoyable (such as using video-chat technology to keep in touch with family members; a favorite pillow to make them feel more comfortable on long bus rides; a sleep sound app on their smartphone to help them get more rest at night; or portable streaming devices and books to keep them occupied on long bus rides).

Putting Things into Perspective
When athletes lack passion for their sport, we can ask them to reflect on what they would be doing had it not been for their talents. Answering this question helps put things into perspective, including where their sport ranks on their list of priorities. When athletes express they have other plans, or want to spend more time with their families, changing their perspective may be more complicated. But when athletes respond, "I don't know, if I wasn't playing maybe I'd be working at a gas station somewhere," we probably have something to work with. Until they have more compelling options, we want athletes to try and appreciate their current status as an athlete. By comparing the benefits of being an athlete to working a regular nine-to-five job, most athletes would agree they are privileged to play sports for a living. I worked with one professional athlete who told me if it wasn't for his talent he would probably be selling insurance somewhere. This athlete understood how fortunate he was to compete in sports for a living. The idea of selling insurance was not appealing to this particular athlete.

Ability to Focus
Before choosing focusing Band-Aid strategies, it is important to consider the nature of an athlete's sport. Different sports may benefit from using different Band-Aids. For sports with continuous action that have fewer interruptions in between, athletes will have fewer opportunities to apply these Band-Aids during competition. For sports with stop-and-go action where each play is separated by pauses, athletes will have more opportunities to apply focusing Band-Aids.

Rapid Eye-Movement
Lately there has been a lot of research regarding rapid eye-movement to facilitate emotional healing. There is even an evidence-based-clinical therapy model called *Eye Movement Desensitization and Reprocessing* (EMDR) which takes advantage of rapid eye-movement and is proven to work. Anecdotally,

I have been told by multiple athletes that using rapid eye-movement on the field helps them mentally regroup and focus quicker. Granted, how athletes use rapid eye-movement will be vastly different from how clinicians use it. But the benefits may be real.

Athletes can use rapid eye-movement to improve focus by picking two objects on the field. These two objects can either be within reach or out of reach, as long as the athlete only uses their eyes to track back-and-forth without moving their head. The athlete starts by briefly focusing on one of the objects until it becomes visibly clear, then quickly shift their line of sight in a straight line onto the other object. Once they visually hone in on the second object and it too becomes clear, they repeat the exercises back-and-forth from one object to the other as quickly as possible, from anywhere between 5-10 seconds continuously.

Examples of two objects athletes can choose from may include: two foul poles in baseball; painted yard lines on a football field; two trees along side a golf course; both ends of the net in tennis; or even by scanning between both hands (or feet) if they are already looking down. Regardless of which two objects athletes choose, we want them to pick things that will maintain a certain level of privacy where others won't notice what they are doing. The more natural athletes appear when they use this strategy, the more privacy they will have.

Since rapid eye-movement requires concentration and controlled eye muscle movements, the strategy may work because it requires the usage of multiple parts of the brain all at the same time. This helps reduce over-thinking, which gives athletes the opportunity to mentally reset. Potentially, it may also be a good exercise to prime vital hand-eye conditioning. If a baseball player is on-deck and the pitcher is throwing 90 mile-per-hour heaters, it's possible the rapid eye-movement exercise can act as a visual warm-up.

Stimulating the Five Senses

When was the last time you went out for a walk and stopped to smell the roses? These days we're so immersed in the distractions around us it's easy for us to lose touch with our surroundings. When athlete's are on the field and are feeling distracted, there is a simple mindfulness technique they can use to harness their focus. I call it *stimulating the five senses*. It is a common clinical technique used to treat people with anxiety and depression and it works big time.

Stimulating the five senses literally involves athletes stopping for a moment by using each of their five senses, each sense up to five times. This includes sight, touch, smell, sound, and taste. This Band-Aid can take up to several minutes to complete in its entirety, but can be condensed into as little as a few seconds. We'll talk about how to shorten the technique in a moment.

The technique typically starts off as the athlete focuses on their vision: to identify five different objects, followed by giving a brief description of each. These objects could be anything inside the stadium or arena, including sports equipment, light fixtures, turf, an empty seat, billboards, the clouds, a fan, etc. For example, a baseball player may look over at the foul pole and notice that it is yellow and tall. Then they may move onto the grass below their feet and comment that it is green and freshly cut. Then they can look at the opposing dugout and notice the manager is taking notes. Then they can look at their cleats and notice they're black with a white swoosh. Then they may look at the infield and notice it's covered in an even layer of dirt. After doing this five times, athletes can move on and repeat the exercise using a different sense the next time.

When athletes use touch during the technique, we want them to physically touch the object they are focusing on. Items to touch can include jerseys, caps, turf, water, hair, skin, a piece of sports equipment, necklace, and so on. For example, a golfer may touch his cap and notice that it is soft. Then they may touch a club and notice it is cold and hard. After touching five different objects, they can move on to the next sense.

The five senses technique continues with athletes trying to notice five different sounds, five different smells, and then five different tastes. Items athletes can listen out for may include fans in the stands, the wind, their teammates, their heartbeat, their opponents, balls flying around, etc. By the time they get to smell and taste, they only need to identify one or two of these senses because they tend to be more limited. Smells may include grass, a piece of sporting equipment, their jersey, a BBQ stand, chlorinated water, etc. Taste on the other hand will be the most limited, but may include sunflower seeds, bubble gum, Gatorade, water, or their saliva.

When athletes don't have enough time to use all five senses, or when using all five senses is too much, they can always focus on just one or two of their senses. If they have even less time they can consider using just one of the senses a few times. As athletes use this strategy, they shouldn't have to walk around to experience a particular sense. Instead they can keep it simple based on what is convenient on the field. There is a lot of flexibility in using this technique.

Focusing on a specific object:

In the 1990's there was a baseball player named Mike Fetters. Many remember Fetters for his unique pitching routine on the mound. Before each pitch, he would take a giant deep breath, stare at the dirt, and after four to six seconds violently swing his head at a 90-degree angle towards the plate before throwing. Watching this routine was entertaining and even bizarre. But for Fetters there was a purpose. He used specks of dirt to help him channel his focus.

Using small objects to channel focus is an increasingly popular strategy that works. It allows athletes to use their surroundings as a tool to clear their heads and tune out all distractions. In a way, this strategy is very similar to the grounding exercise we discussed in chapter three. Except this focusing Band-Aid doesn't involve studying an object's characteristics. Instead, this Band-Aid simply uses staring at a tiny object as a point of reference until athletes feel focused and mentally prepared.

Objects to choose from should be small enough that athletes have to focus intently to spot them. Finding small objects helps minimize internal thoughts as athletes are forced to concentrate real hard onto an object. Objects to choose from should be accessible throughout the entire game, meaning they will not unexpectedly disappear as the game goes on (such as a distant fan sitting in their seat). This way, athletes can rely on using the same object throughout the game. Examples of objects athletes may consider include: a scuff on the tennis court; a blade of grass; a freckle on one's hand; the tip of a shoelace; etc.

Here are several examples how athletes may use small specific objects to channel their focus. For best results it helps when athletes use the same objects routinely and consistently because the familiarity of that item may promote emotional comfort.

A baseball player can draw a teeny-tiny dot on their bat with a Sharpie marker. Before each swing on deck and in between pitches, the athlete spins the bat in their hands, directs their focus onto locating that small dot, finds it, and stares at it for several seconds until they feel mentally set.

A basketball player can pick a wooden slat on the court before free-throws, or stare at the exact spot where they want the ball to go while using positive imagery.

A golfer can focus on a divot on a golf ball as it sits on a tee before a drive, and as they concentrate on taking slow, deep breaths.

A tennis player can focus on a scuff near the service line before each serve.

Sing a Song, Think of Something Funny

On some occasions external influences such as a hostile crowd, or a recent mistake, can make us upset and thus make it harder to concentrate. The more attention we pay to these distractions, the more we lose our focus. In these cases singing a favorite song in our head, or thinking of something funny (including something that may have happened to us earlier in the week) can help us focus away from these distractions and onto something more pleasant. If the funny memory (or joke) is really funny, it can take even more pressure off of our minds. Furthermore, remember the ABC's of "Thought

Stopping" in chapter four? This could be a great *'change the thought'* once an athlete becomes aware of a thought and BAMS it.

Explore Extracurricular Focusing Activities
There are always additional activities off the field athletes can participate in to sharpen their focusing skills. These activities require focus as a part of the experience. Examples of extracurricular activities athletes can partake in include: yoga; meditation; art classes; and music lessons. Legendary NBA coach Phil Jackson used Zen Mindfulness with his teams while coaching for the Bulls and Lakers. Although Zen Mindfulness may have seemed like a foreign approach to his players, they reported that it was actually quite useful in promoting focus during games.

Final Words:
Over the years I have been privileged to witness the growth in my athletes. There is nothing more satisfying than watching them knock on your door desperate for help, only to come out with a renewed sense of confidence that is real. Many of my clients have pulled themselves out of the mud and lead meaningful careers. Some have overachieved and exceeded even their own expectations. Others came in with sound mental skills, emerging stronger than ever before. And several have gone on to fulfill their dreams by reaching the highest levels within their sport. You now have the knowledge and information to get the same results out of your athletes.

As I mentioned in the intro, your role with athletes will determine how you apply mental performance enhancement tools. I encourage everyone to get creative when applying SPET tools because the possibilities are endless. Don't be afraid to get creative by mixing-and-matching different tools, thereby creating customized plans depending on individual athlete's needs. Take *The Art of SPET* information and run with it. Here are some ways coaches and sports professionals may apply SPET strategies into their own practice:

Team coaches: Along with offering specific tools to individual players, coaches can tailor "mini-packages" for each player depending on their needs. Using the mix-and-match approach, coaches can concoct individualized formulas. For example, they may tell an athlete to "BAP," which can be an acronym for Breathe, show Attitude, and Poise control. Or a player may "APP," which is an acronym for Attitude, Poise control, and Positive imagery. Or they may "GPF," Grounding, Positive self-talk, Focus. Again, these are just some examples. You can use your ingenuity to come up with bigger and better ideas.

Team coaches additionally have the option to apply the steps of SPET using a team format. This will not only save coaches a lot of time and energy, it will also produce fantastic results. For example, coaches may start off a team meeting by discussing goal setting and flags one week; followed by deep breathing and muscle relaxation the following week; positive self-talk the third week; poise control the fourth week; and positive imagery the fifth week. Anecdotally, when entire teams utilize the same skills, I have noticed team dynamics get stronger as athletes naturally start to encourage and pull for each other more.

Other ways sports professionals may take advantage of SPET information include: a personal trainer teaching athletes to use deep breathing, positive self-talk, and positive imagery to find their runner's high quicker; a strength and conditioning coach telling an athlete to use deep breathing, positive imagery, and the 'locate a small object' focusing Band-Aid before attempting to break their deadlift record; or a scout/recruiter asking an athlete's coach, teammates, or parents about their training regime to gauge their commitment and dedication towards their sport. No matter your relationship with athletes, it is up to you to decide how SPET can help you and your athletes the most.

Over time the field of sporty psychology will continue to grow and evolve. Old strategies may one day become obsolete, as revolutionary new strategies and technologies replace them over time. For those who are interested and are passionate about our field, I challenge you to reach for new discoveries and share them with the sports community so athletes everywhere will benefit. We should take great pride in our work. The athlete is why we do what we do. This is for them.